gardening 101

PAUL THOMPSON

PAUL THOMPSON

SPECIAL PHOTOGRAPHY BY ANDREA JONES

garden

4

For Kirsten and Rumi

Gardening 101

Copyright © Frances Lincoln Limited 2001

Text and artwork copyright

© Paul Thompson 2001

Photographs copyright © Frances Lincoln

Limited except for those listed on page 192.

First published in the UK as *Virgin Gardener*

by Frances Lincoln Limited

This edition published by

TODTRI Book Publishers

254 West 31st Street

New York, NY 10001-2813

Fax: (212) 695-6984

E-mail: info@todtri.com

Visit us on the web!

www.todtri.com

ISBN 1-57717-197-7

Contents

Introduction

A year ago, spurred on by impending parenthood, I moved with my partner Kirsten to a country cottage which came with the challenge of a partially overgrown and unkempt rural plot – a situation not dissimilar to the one you may now be facing. Our virgin ground comprised a large, spring-fed pond at its far end, the ruins of an outbuilding in the middle and land running behind and in front of the cottage itself. It seemed a decent size without being too big. I was excited as to what wonders we might perform here.

On my first midwinter stroll outdoors to contemplate creative wizardry, I became rapidly confused, my mind whirring with images of terraces, romantic topiary, ornamental parterres with surreal sculptures – all either beyond budget or feasibility. With a mind full of mirages, I retreated indoors for a week or so and glared at the garden, while it glared back at me. I then tried again, this time with a more measured approach. With lofty ambitions of aesthetic conquest now laid aside, I surveyed the garden afresh and began making decisions based on common sense and practicality. I looked at each individual area, and devised down-to-earth solutions that were led by the garden, rather than imposed on it.

Behind the picket fence, between the house and the lane, you would expect to find a typical cottage garden – all show for passers-by. Going with this theme, we decided to distil its essence into a random collection of tall, vertical herbaceous perennials – a kind of flowering frenzy. We had brought with us just one item of furniture, a huge seat, nicknamed the Giant's Rest, built to outsized proportions, but where to put it? The garden itself presented us with a perfect location, backing on to a hedge between a large maple tree and a small flowering cherry; the seat nestled between the two trunks as if made to measure.

We decided to leave a large grassy bank, bristling with nettles, between the pond and the outbuilding as a reminder of the garden's former wildness, as well as a habitat for creatures and insects. However, on the other side of this ruin, behind the house, was a spot that begged for cultivation. Here, a raised section of grass had most of the day's sun, as well as the protection of the ruin: a perfect enclosure for an ornamental vegetable garden. To make up for poor, rubble-filled soil, we created a patterned layout of timber-edged raised beds curving around a central circle formed from upended and semi-buried coloured glass bottles.

As spring progressed and the beds started to fill with foliage, our appetite for plants overflowed into fifty or so terracotta and black plastic pots. We even bartered sturdy plastic fish-boxes from a fisherman and planted them with tomatoes and runner beans. We watched as first flowers, then fruits started to appear. With the onset of such delights came a run-in with the local slugs that saw me become a ruthless executioner of these slimy devourers – dashing them against the brick paths for the birds.

Now that our first summer in the garden is drawing to a close, the early days of wrangling with lofty and unsuitable ideas seem a long way off. Having arrived with a desire to conquer and impose, I have learned the value of accepting the will of a raggedy plot that only needed its surface scratched to perform wonders. And the Giant's Rest is regularly crowded with our new family (plus dogs) at sunset, where we plan additions and alterations for next year – with the garden's permission, of course.

PAUL THOMPSON

seeking inspiration

The unexploited territory of a virgin plot, or a garden gone to seed, holds great potential for creative transformation. A garden of your own presents you with infinite possible combinations of plants, materials, features and styles and the challenge of finding a grouping that feels right for you. This book will help you to seek out that combination and show you how to put it together.

In this first chapter we look at a variety of sources for the inspirational spark that will begin the design process. A good starting point – long before you lay a path or even commit a design to paper – is to investigate the contents and layout of your garden. Look at such fixed aspects as the size, location and orientation of the plot itself as well as thinking about how you will use it and the styles, colours and textures that will characterize it.

The aim is to help you create a picture, through a methodical refinement of your thoughts and their possible manifestations, of a layout and a core of ingredients that will become the framework for your garden. The actual process of design is not a daunting one – it involves a series of steps that are covered in more detail on pages 114–27. But before this can happen, you need to take time to find a 'way in' that will spark off the ultimate design, leading you through the maze of possibilities to a garden that is personal to you. By following this chapter you increase the chance for personal inspiration to become the basis of your design. This is, however, only the start: what you find in the course of these early investigations is without doubt important but it is no more than a beginning. The full picture has still to develop and be fleshed out.

Using the space

'What do you want from your garden?' is the first question I ask a new client. The answer is normally a wish list that can range from the modest to the impossible. But whatever the response, getting this information is a vital early stage in conjuring the image of a garden that will reflect the personality and style of its owner. It's good to be clear about how you will ultimately use your garden before you start to divide up the space and work with it. These early thoughts can also help, in later stages, to guide the design process.

Make a list of ways in which you will use the garden in order of importance and notice how each one brings forth a separate design consideration. You may, for instance, be keen on eating outdoors – this will require an even surface such as a terrace or patio, possibly in close proximity to the house. There might also be an emphasis on family use and children's play, in which case you will need to have plenty of clear space – perhaps a lawn – along with protected or robust planting. If you live in an urban environment and want a garden in which to escape, you might need to obscure the immediate surroundings with screening plants, trellis or fencing. Plants and features may have to be large and dominant to create a sense of enclosure and to focus attention within the garden.

Many people want a garden to be an extension of their living space. These 'outdoor rooms' can be sumptuous or simple, depending on the type of room they extend. A garden laid out for relaxation will need provision for seating and lounging, arranged within a layout whose lines and features combine to reflect harmony. If the garden is to be the site of a work place, such as a shed or studio, consider the building's size and whether it will become central to the layout or will need to be obscured at any cost.

Perhaps you crave a highly productive yet ornamental vegetable garden that will feed your family and be a pleasant place in which to relax as well as toil. In this case a sunny aspect, fertile soil, storage space and some protection from damaging winds, such as hedges or fencing, may be required. If a swimming pool and a hot tub appear high on your list, consider budget – and what may have to be sacrificed in favour of such expensive features.

The way in which you will use your garden has a great influence on the ultimate design. Here, 'outdoor living' characterizes a broad raised deck with ample space for table and chairs, where meals can be enjoyed in natural surroundings.

Where might they be placed? Will you make them the main focus of the garden or, if not, do you have enough space to conceal them? Are there any overhanging trees that may cause unwanted shade or drop leaves to clog filters and tarnish water? By relating such wishes to the site you can invest your

list with some down-to-earth realities that may help with selection at this stage. Then again, you may be realizing that you want all of the above and more. If so, you have some important prioritizing to do. Look at the available space and try to see how you can combine your various needs. A pragmatic approach will serve you well, but great results can also be achieved from cramming in as much as is humanly possible – for an example, take a look at the tiny garden shown on pages 50–51.

Incorporated around a curved central pathway are areas for children to play in and space for a table and chairs, with varied perennial planting and structural use of evergreen topiary shapes to complement stone features. With its many possible uses, this garden maintains a visual unity.

Identifying the conditions

A few years ago I designed and built a garden on the shores of a lake in southern Switzerland. Not being familiar with the climatic and soil conditions of an alpine region, I spent valuable hours at the beginning of the project driving round and looking at mature gardens in the locality. I gleaned a mass of information about the sort of materials in common use and the variety of plants that flourished despite heavy winter snows and sharp frosts. These visible clues gave me instant knowledge; I benefited from years of trial and error and hard work on the part of the local gardening fraternity. So always allow neighbouring gardeners to burden you with the benefit of their experience. One day, you may be leaning over a fence doing the same.

The location and orientation of your garden will also give an early indication of what you will be able to achieve with plants and materials and what might be appropriate in terms of design. The way the garden faces will dictate the availability of sunlight and shade which will affect the siting of plants and seating areas. So walk out in your garden on bright and overcast days to study the effect of light and shadow. Follow the pattern of sunlight throughout the day to see where sun-loving plants might thrive and observe the shadows cast by trees, boundaries or structures for the siting of shade-loving plants.

If you are in an urban location, with a backdrop

A raised open site such as this roof terrace benefits from exposure to sun but must also deal with driving winds and rain. The formal design solution is a generous deck with robust planting and simple architecture that takes advantage of the stark light and shadows on a hot day to conjure up a seductive garden scene.

of buildings – which often reflect a sense of neutrality – you may welcome the opportunity this gives to opt for a strong design and diverse dramatic planting that might jar in a more natural rural setting. A city or town will also have warmer air – due to lighting, heating and traffic fumes trapped within and around buildings – than surrounding rural areas and will support more delicate plants in unprotected situations.

Local weather conditions will indicate maximum and minimum temperatures and rainfall throughout the year, as well as how much sun you are likely to enjoy and whether strong winds are a problem. A garden on a roof or at the brow of a hill could be exposed to drying winds or intense summer sun, so consider the provision of barriers, windbreaks and shade, and select drought- and wind-tolerant plant species. On the coast, a milder, frost-free climate might allow you to grow more tender exotics; on the other hand, biting salt winds could be a problem, together with shallow topsoil and constant surface erosion. Again, think about providing barriers or limit the planting to tough, stunted plants.

The type of soil in the landscape – be it clay, loam, sandy or stony – will indicate suitable plants (see the individual entries in the Plant manifesto, pages 162–89). And though, with the application of fertilizers, soil conditioners, drainage and irrigation, conditions can be improved, there are situations where certain plants will not thrive. Look at the structure of your soil: if it is dry, gritty and loose, then drought-tolerant and aromatic plants, used to such conditions, should guide your plant selection. If, on the other hand, it holds moisture and is rich in organic matter, this situation will favour large-leaved, shade-tolerant plants and 'marginals' used to having their roots in water.

In this small coastal garden an exotic planting acts as a canopy of foliage to provide shade from intense summer sun for its owners. These distinctive plants not only afford shelter but create an intentionally private garden with a jungle feel and great visual impact.

It is also worth carrying out a test to assess the pH level of your soil, that is, its acidity or alkalinity. This is done with a small kit (easily purchased from a garden centre) and the information it provides will again signal different plant selections. The majority of camellias and rhododendrons will only grow on acidic soil, for example, whereas lilac and hebes prefer an alkaline, chalky soil. If you are going to spend a lot of money on mature trees and shrubs, you may wish to have a full laboratory test of your soil carried out.

Observation

It is an instinctive response to want to clear an overgrown garden, to chop it all back and then think about a new design. But delay this process if you can, as it may lead to a hasty destruction of useful clues. An old shed might indicate an ideal position for an elaborate timber summer house, studio or pergola. Clumps of weeds or the overgrown remnants from a former garden could help you decide on the siting, shape and proportions of lush, deep borders filled with flowering perennials and grasses. A thicket of self-seeded saplings and shrubs might be transformed into a glade of ornamental trees or a minimal block of coppiced hazel – a dense, geometric design feature doubling as a habitat for birds and mammals. Try to think expansively and to reconsider – in terms of shapes, textures and tones – what you might too readily have dismissed as rubbish.

Take a good look at the site of your new garden: hidden within its contents and composition, however rudimentary, there may be elements that will assist and influence you in your search for a design. If the plot is empty, you face the challenge of a blank canvas: this can be intimidating but it also offers the luxury of unfettered possibilities. There will always be something there to influence you, however, even if it is merely a boundary fence – what it is made of, its length, the amount of snade it casts or the light it catches can all start you thinking. In a part-filled space there is a beginning, and be it a tree, shrub, wall or structure, this can give you a clue that signposts the whole design process. Equally, it can lead to hours of agonizing about impossible symmetry or inappropriate colour or texture if it is something that cannot be moved. Aim to work around

immutable items from the earliest stage, to acknowledge their presence and to devise ways in which they can become part of the design.

When you go out into the garden, be aware of those places where you often pause; this might be the site for a terrace with furniture or just a quiet corner with a simple seat. Make a note of important views that might become vistas that you frame with a row of trees, an arch or pergola. Look at the garden from as many vantage points as possible, for example from an upstairs window, to see if any hidden patterns might reveal themselves within tree canopies, shapes in the grass or formations, such as mounds or hummocks, in the soil. Any of these might become a significant factor and guide your design from an early stage. Take the time to document both what you uncover in your own garden and also the variety of possible uses suggested to you by the areas and conditions you find there. This will become part of an initial framework for your design.

You may be surprised at a much later stage when, on completion of your garden, you study photographs of the site before work started. In my experience I have often noticed that shapes, patterns, even tones and textures from a neglected garden have subliminally made their creative mark in my designs. So even if things don't leap out at you for reinterprertation or reuse, it is still worth spending time observing your site to allow for more subtle influences to take place.

This small back garden that I transformed for a client made an important impression on me from the beginning. I reinterpreted a change of level leading to a patchy lawn (seen in the 'before' picture, left) as a step up to a tiled terrace surrounded by raised timber-edged beds (seen below). The large mophead hydrangea on the right, one of only a few original plants, was too big to move into the raised beds, so I brought its curving profile into the new garden, along with a sculptural cloud-pruned evergreen privet, the owner's favourite plant.

Personal inspiration

If you find yourself still seeking inspiration after studying the plot itself, then take your quest indoors. The home is, for many, a less intimidating and alien environment than the wilds of 'out there'. We are all familiar with the idea of living in rooms and most of us create our indoor sanctuaries around personal preferences – be it with reed mats, incense holders, futon and bamboo screens or with chintz cushions, pelmets, carved furniture and oil paintings. Whatever the contents and arrangement of our interiors, they tell a story of how we respond to space. And creating an interior is not unlike designing a garden, except that it's a little easier to move furniture around than to re-locate a summer house!

So look at your favourite room and establish what you like about it. Here, perhaps, are some of your favourite colours, along with materials, textures and the kind of furniture you favour, all of which convey your style. Notice how furniture is placed within the room – is the arrangement formal and geometric or does it break the room up into random areas? Do you fill rooms with colourful clutter or keep them sparse and clear? If you strive for uncluttered space indoors, you may want a garden that feels the same.

If you live in a striking minimalist home, where features are unified by geometry and strong lines, you may favour a garden with pared-down features and simplified block planting. Or cabin fever may induce a need for carefree chaos.

Look to your artwork for signs, clues, colours and patterns. Here the graphic interlinked circles in a wall hanging could be the springboard for an exciting decorative design in an ornamental vegetable garden, parterre or rose garden.

Of course you will not be trying to reproduce your interior room outside, but studying it may well give you a clue that starts a landslide of ideas. Such information came to my rescue while designing an ornamental vegetable garden for a young family. We had all agreed on a garden of organic vegetables with fruit trees, climbers and flowers, but had not found a pattern to govern the layout of beds and pathways. A piece of Indian textile on a wall indoors caught my eye, and within its complex patterns I noticed a tiny square with the proportions of the intended garden, within which were two concentric circles bisected by lines at right angles. This not only became the layout of beds and paths but the purple dye in the cloth featured strongly in the planting's ultimate colour scheme. This small discovery had inspired the design.

If indoors still leaves you uninspired, look through your photograph albums for cultural references – colours, tones or textures – that convey to you a style. Think of a favourite destination or landscape that has entranced you: the lavender fields of Provence, the rich red of a sunset at Ayers Rock, the arid natural minimalism of the New Mexico deserts or the lush exotic islands in the Indian Ocean. If you have learned to love gardens partly through the planted areas in your local park, take a walk and see what planting combinations, methods of enclosure or other ideas you might be able to reinterpret and apply to your own patch.

If your quest for inspiration takes you beyond your home, then try looking through your holiday snaps. An image of a favourite beach, town, village, hotel – even a coloured wall or a market scene – may trigger your design. The arid landscape pictured above might suggest a limited palette of complementary greens and oranges or it may point you towards a bold, desert-style planting or even suggest an awe-inspiring earth sculpture.

Deciding what to keep

Many people work to the rule that, when you start afresh in a garden, you should remove anything that you are not totally passionate about. This can be a sensible approach provided you have checked with relevant planning departments, tree and conservation officers as to any protected status that may govern your plans. But the desire to start with a clean slate must be tempered by considering the possible value of what you propose removing. If it is a majestic mature tree, for instance, with character, a strong sculptural presence and a wealth of wildlife, think long and hard before you seek to remove what nature has taken years to create. If, on the other hand, it's an old, rotten shed, then get out the sausages and

A gentle monochromatic leafy structure has infiltrated the space around these mature trees. Their presence has been utilized in this design to give a sense of natural enclosure and to focus gently on a skilfully placed ornament that makes a perfect tonal contrast to its surroundings.

make that bonfire! Never underestimate the value of mature plants and old structures which create a sense of time past in a new garden and speed the 'settling in' process by softening the impact of fresh additions and giving scale to a garden full of immature young plants. It is best to identify precisely what elements you wish to keep and what will have to stay quite early on, so that this gets taken into consideration from the beginning. Whatever you decide to keep must inevitably become integral to, and may even take over, your design, if these elements are not to live in conflict with what you create.

While caution must be exercised to avoid any wanton destruction, it is important that you do not become intimidated if you inherit a substantial and impressive garden. If you are dazzled by the glare of what someone else has made, you may feel that you can't change anything. If its contents are a treasure trove of delights that will harmonize with, and even enhance, your personal design, then you are indeed lucky. More often, the opposite is the case – where an old pergola, a conifer-encrusted island bed or a large tree seem rigorously opposed to the ideal of your design. Always try to look at elements creatively and you may find that you can devise ways of turning obstacles into positive features.

Having explored all possible sources for personal inspiration and, hopefully, discovered for yourself a context or an idea that will help you to stamp your personality on your new garden, it is time to roam beyond the confines of your plot for a while and relish delights others have achieved. In the next chapter – Visualizing your dream – give your imagination leave to fly off into the world of beautifully designed gardens. You may pick up further details and features that could give life to

In my own garden the wall of an old ruined outhouse, which happens to receive most of the day's sunlight, provides a colourful backdrop to a seat from which to contemplate thriving vegetables and companion plants. A vine and a clematis that we also inherited are encouraged to form a shaded arch that will provide welcome respite from the sun's rays.

your garden. Using the images and text as a guide, borrow ideas that seem appropriate and reinvent them within – or alongside – the design ideas that have inspired you so far. This begins the process of fleshing out the bones of your own design.

visualizing your dream

In the portfolio of inspiring gardens on the following pages you will be able to study the heights and delights of what others have created and absorb what they have achieved. Before you have created a garden, your expectations of what might be realized may well be far lower than what is actually possible. So don't hold back. You now have a good idea of the physical and geographical limitations that come with your site and an outline of how you want to use it. With all this to anchor you, it's time to seek some stimulating ideas. Feel free to take what you will from the gardens illustrated – any detail or combination of themes, plants or materials can be yours. Just keep referring back to your initial ideas and any framework you may have drawn up, for a reality check, then go off in search of inspiration again. Keep this process going, making additions and subtractions until a design begins to emerge – anything that is not right should naturally fall by the wayside at some point during the process.

As you will see, many successful gardens result from the tension between extravagant dreams and practical reality. Ideas and concepts are constantly refined until they will just fit within the constraints and confines of the garden they are destined for. And to unite these extremes of aesthetic ambition and earth-bound reality into a dynamic balance you must resist compromise. It is most important at this stage that you do not give up your dream too easily and risk missing out on some of the really exciting possibilities for your garden.

Key types of garden design

Over the following fifty-six pages, a portfolio of garden themes is presented, comprising pleasing, inspired and workable gardens. Each reflects a particular approach and, sometimes, a specific culture, geography and climate, with their own relevant plants and features, all of which help to define different styles, as well as embellishing and adding character to them. Today, cultural exchange and the widespread export of plants sees exotic-looking varieties being selected for their ability to withstand cooler climates, so we can adopt – and adapt – many of these styles, even those that originated in far-off places, and enjoy their benefits within our own gardens.

I have selected twelve key types of garden, to give a broad picture of the wide range of possible designs, and each is headed by a summary of its typical characteristics. The styles described and depicted here are intended to offer inspiration and stimulation, to help you bring substance and unity to the ideas you have settled on so far and to accommodate your needs in a creative manner. Seeking a theme can be a great help as a way of beginning to assemble a range of disparate ideas into a harmonious whole. If you are drawn to a particular design, this can help guide your choices. Your aim is not to copy or replicate wholesale, but to draw inspiration from the gardens illustrated, to assimilate aspects of them with your own ideas and to identify those elements that might have a specific appeal or relevance to you in your own garden design.

To help you see how different themes might be adapted and plundered for your own use, some are accompanied by a pair of drawings (these are also shown here on the right). For these illustrations I have selected two very different garden situations, one large and open and one enclosed, both with existing features of their own, such as trees, shrubs, walls and fences. Where the type of design I'm discussing – for example, formal style – relies on certain specific principles that govern layout and other such visual considerations, I have sketched into the plots a possible layout and features showing how a particular style might be imposed on each of them. By this means, I hope to give you some idea of the different ways in which you might tackle the interpretation of these inspiring styles and beautiful gardens in your own plot.

The open site

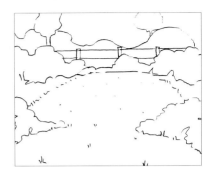

The enclosed site

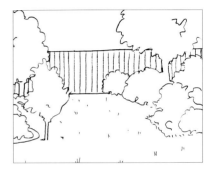

formal

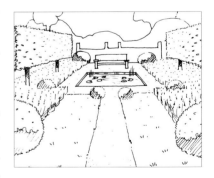

carefree

exotic

potager

minimal

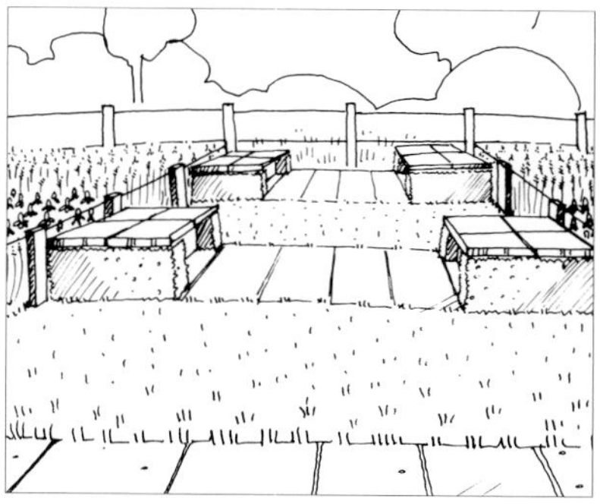

romantic

fusion

- ◆ Geometric proportions

- ◆ Symmetrical planting

- ◆ Clean lines

- ◆ A sense of control

- ◆ Plants clipped as structure

formal

The parallel lines of a timber deck set the scene for this stylish urban roof terrace where formality has been skilfully applied. Through a well-proportioned, symmetrical arrangement of containerized Japanese maples and box balls, along with simple furniture and ornament of a spare, bold design, the garden presents a calm and inviting extension of the conservatory's interior.

A formal garden is a highly controlled environment, which influences the way in which it is enjoyed. Through a strongly delineated geometric layout and the deliberate, usually symmetrical, placement of both plants and features, we are told where to sit, how to move about the garden and where to stop and pause to contemplate views and focal points. Such an inflexible approach reflects the designer's passion for architecture and dominance over nature and ensures that the visitor is unlikely to miss anything important in their experience of such a garden.

Planting is stylized into geometric shapes, with trees and shrubs often clipped into topiary pieces and architectural structures, such as hedges and screens. Repeat planting, in rows or pairs, is another distinguishing feature. Along with straight paths and other structural elements, the plants guide us through the garden and provide a framework within which seating areas, settings for sculpture, rectilinear water channels, as well as openings for views, are located.

While the formal style originated in tiny Roman courtyard gardens and was later seen in the gardens of medieval castles and moated manor houses, it really flourished in the very large spaces of the grand Renaissance gardens. In the sixteenth century it served to compartmentalize the vast estates and parklands of the chateaux of France and the villas of Italy. The secret of designing a formal garden in a large space is to divide it up and give the eye points of reference. Sometimes a pattern is chosen that fits the entire space and is then repeated within itself: a square divided into four squares, say, with each of these divided into four again, and so on. By this means, large areas are fragmented via gentle geometry into spaces that are more human in scale – down to a tiny bed with four blocks of different varieties of lavender. The grand formal gardens of the past were in fact designed to be enjoyed from the house windows, where their detail would have appeared smaller and more intricate than their true scale.

Formal style relies on an architectural approach and uses internal divisions and external boundaries to define the garden's layout. These boundaries are most often designated by hedges of clipped evergreens such as yew, box and laurel, for structures that will remain through the winter, along with faster-growing deciduous versions in hornbeam

and beech. Within the garden, raised hedges of hornbeam or lime might further serve to create a sense of geometric enclosure. Structures such as walls, trellis, fences and screens also help with this demarcation of the garden. Beds are often edged with low hedges to prevent the planting spilling over on to paths and walkways. Within them, small plants such as lavender and other herbs may be arranged in blocks, sometimes within the confines of box-edged parterres (small patterned planting areas).

The paths and structures that describe the garden's layout should reflect the geometry and order of the formal style, while the ambitious choice of exciting new materials can give it a contemporary

The placement of an elaborate topiary feature between two doorways (above) decorates the formal symmetry of this quiet corner of a garden. Different areas of the same garden (right) are interlinked through a geometric arrangement of clipped evergreen hedges and obelisks. A rill flows into a rectangular pool surrounded by gravel leading the eye to a raised seating area beyond. The golden ball in the pool creates an elaborate focus in a key area.

interpretation – a modern design can be striking within a style that has its roots so firmly fixed in the history of gardens. Paths and terraces made from sawn stone, decking, tiles, bricks or concrete will echo the lines and symmetry of the garden. Placed within this framework, furniture made from wood, stone or metal should be uniform with clean lines. Features like ponds and fountains made from stone or glass, as well as containers and trellis of galvanized or stainless steel, will further strengthen a contemporary look. Try to integrate these features with one another, choosing for visual compatibility.

Formality can have a striking modern application in a garden of any size, big or small, or even in a window box. The sense of order inherent in a formal design can help a small or enclosed garden appear larger. It is important to select a layout pattern that best fits the shape of your plot, so the underlying design will work, with no odd shapes to reduce its strength. For example, in a rectangular garden, the layout might be based on a rectangle or two squares. Look for opportunities to echo the pattern in the smallest of details, such as the arrangement of bricks on a terrace, in the design of your seating or the detail on trellis.

The success of formality is underpinned by keeping gardens smart and immaculate in appearance, so bear in mind the time required for the maintenance of trees and shrubs that may need regular clipping to preserve a good outline, as well as the hours devoted to keeping the garden pristine.

As with all styles, the formal style is open to interpretation. Some of the materials mentioned are expensive and may require skilled labour, but if these are beyond your budget, don't be put off. With a little lateral thought, you can establish a strong formal style in any garden, and still benefit from its clean lines and refined order, whether made from glass and steel or from less refined ingredients such as reclaimed timber. Whatever you use to build your garden, keep everything in it true to the linear design round which it was formed.

INTERPRETING FORMAL STYLE

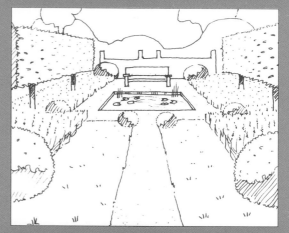

- Open vista flanked by clipped, raised hedges
- Broad beds filled with unfussy planting, perhaps a single herb
- Clipped topiary balls create a foil for straight lines
- Rectangular pool a key structural feature

- Small tree surrounded by 4 benches as central focus
- Uniform stone paving slabs laid in regular pattern
- Symmetrical planting enclosed by rear and side screening to retain visual formality

conceptual

♦ Strong themes ♦ Original use of materials ♦ Focus on form rather than function

♦ Subjective design ideas ♦ Concepts pushed to their extreme

The design and layout of a garden are led by inspirational ideas and key themes. These ideas – be they a colour, shape or texture (see Seeking inspiration, page 16) – help to build the image of a design, lending it character and giving substance to the final composition. Often they make their contribution then quietly recede behind the overall impression of planting and detail that embellishes the original idea. The constraints of actually making a garden can modify the impact of a design as it contends with the realities of materials, plant sizes and shapes and true colours, and many gardens turn out to be quite different from what the initial concept promised. In this way a garden develops a life of its own, away from the pencilled lines and grids of its origin.

Conceptual gardens, however, make no such compromises. Like all conceptual art, they challenge the viewer and often subvert the way we look at our environment by presenting it to us in unfamiliar ways. There is usually a subtext to the initial visual experience, for example in a garden strewn with text-inscribed features or based on complex molecular patterns. We are required to study these gardens, to work hard to understand their hidden meanings and to open our minds to new ways of using gardens. In a conceptual garden plants may be replaced by rods of steel or illuminated fluorescent tubes, and a lawn is as likely to be made from a poured section of dyed concrete with texture scored into its wet surface as it is of grass; a pool of water may, on inspection, be a sheet of black glass.

While conceptual gardens can be dazzling and exciting places, they can, at the same time, be perplexing and uncomfortable. Wit and humour, or simply a sense of the weird, may be the driving force behind their creation. A garden in which all features and plants are black, or where varnished bagels delineate a path made of purple gravel, will be sublime to some and anathema to others.

Conceptual gardens that express strongly held ideas are generally pushed to their extreme for maximum effect. There are no specific ingredients, but what

Designer Martha Schwartz plays with our perceptions of how a garden should look in this challenging arrangement of 'rooms' and use of striking colours. Plants like cacti (above) and a sculptural pyramid of stone shards (right) are each presented within their own enclosure.

characterizes these gardens is the way in which their contents are treated. A circle and the proportions of a circle may, for example, be the chosen concept, in which case circular planting areas with round-leaved perennials (such as *Ligularia dentata* 'Desdemona'), circular lawns and seating areas, and galvanized cylindrical containers could all be a manifestation of that idea. Wherever you look, you see the circle at work, in different sizes and proportions.

The curved dry-stone walls, mounds of earth and stone cairns of land artists like Andy Goldsworthy are a great source of inspiration for a garden whose concept centres on a reworking of natural elements. Often inspired by art and architecture, conceptual gardens can seem to be neither garden, nor building, nor structure. As a setting for sculpture, a conceptual garden may actually take on the attributes of the art so that it becomes a sculpture in itself and no longer merely a place of entertainment and horticultural enterprise. The sky can become your garden, with a lawn encircled by trees the only elements needed for you to be able to lie down and gaze up at an ever-changing skyscape, fringed by foliage. You might devise a stellar garden where silver foliage plants and structures of glass, stainless steel and mirror are illuminated to dazzle at night.

These subjective, dramatic gardens challenge the confines of taste: you are as free as you want to be from the aesthetic constraints that serve to define other styles, such as scale and proportion, balance and colour sense.

In a San Francisco garden plants pay homage to the sparkling purity of mounded ground glass cones that rise serenely through a pool of still water. With a surrounding 'mulch' of blue glass these unlikely colours and textures invest the plants with a frozen, almost synthetic presence, that has its own beauty and is reminiscent of the atmospheric tranquillity in a dry Zen garden.

Maverick designer Ivan Hicks uses found objects such as ridge tiles, trellis posts and a ladder along with concrete statues of Grecian high priestesses and combines them with hazel 'cobwebs' to create an evocative enchanted forest.

Many of us have an image of our dream garden, but while these visions often remain out of reach, locked in our wildest dreams, they can still lead us forward in our quest for outdoor perfection.

As gardens are often more or less free from the major building constraints of our homes – such as structural limitations and planning laws – they beg the creation of something imaginative, unfettered and very personal. With such freedom at our fingertips, dreams really can be made to come true. The inspiration for a fantasy garden can come from literature, music, childhood memories or the visions of your children: the scope is endless. Whatever the dream, story or theme around which you wish to create your garden, you must keep it in mind at all times and take every opportunity to convey it. As long as you remain excited by the possible outcome and do not shy away from the weird and the wonderful, fantasy gardens offer the power, mystery and delight of the imagination within a framework of reality.

In a fantasy garden decoration and design may well override function. Contents are chosen for their ability to convey an unusual atmosphere and are often assembled to make evocative, symbolic, even surreal arrangements. For instance, large and small topiary pieces might be juxtaposed to bring about altered perspectives, elaborate woven shapes of hazel and willow constructed to provide

fantasy

♦ Fantastical themes ♦ Mystical shapes and magical figures ♦ Places of escape
♦ Dramatic and imaginative planting ♦ Allusion to childhood

support for plants, and buildings such as summer houses or follies built to a diminished scale to exaggerate the size of large plants surrounding them. Such features might be incorporated in a layout based on strong patterns, such as spirals, webs and circles, which can be embodied by earth mazes and winding pathways that entwine with one another. The resulting creations are beautiful, mystifying and strangely fantastical places which expand our perceptions of what a garden should look like.

If your fantasy garden is to be geared towards children, think back to what seemed most magical when you were a child. Use scale and proportion to distort reality and introduce decoration wherever possible. If you have large trees, build a tree house

or two; turn a glade of saplings into an enchanted woodland with the simple addition of wind chimes, mobiles, mirrors and flags attached to branches. Use bright, stimulating colours, not only on structures but also in the plants you choose. Sun-flowers are always a favourite, not only for their cheerful flowers but also for the extraordinary

This garden at the San Diego Children's Hospital has a reassuring sense of protection within its layout of bright, gently curving walls. Designer Topher Delaney erodes any sense of 'containment' through a wealth of fun and fantasy in the lively planes of colour on walls and floor and large objects such as a mosaic star (right) with smooth, curved edges for seating and play. She creates an imaginative space for play and learning – suitable for reinterpretation in an enclosed urban plot – whose whimsical embellishment of animal figures acts as a stimulus for youthful imaginations.

growth that occurs between seed stage and a 3m/10ft tall bloom in one summer. Choose soft surfaces over hard – such as grass and shredded bark in place of stone slabs, and timber instead of brick – and banish all sharp corners and edges from your design. Plants are likely to come in for a bashing so choose robust varieties and protect them in raised beds or with low fences. Such structures can be given a colourful and decorative finish, too, so they are seen as a more prominent feature in the garden. Always avoid poisonous,

thorny and irritant plants: nurseries and other suppliers should be able to advise you about these.

Gardens are an enriching part of childhood. They are places where young minds are free to roam and invent all manner of possibilities, where trees and shrubs become the denizens of lost worlds and a pile of soil a castle or fortress. Fantasy gardens allow us to rediscover this rich imaginative experience as we create spaces that transport us back to our own childhood or forward into the land of adult dreams.

♦ Natural materials

♦ Relaxed approach

♦ Blurred boundaries

♦ Native plant species

carefree

Drawing us away from the desire to control and organize our lives, the permissive, informal atmosphere of a carefree style offers the enchantment of a garden in which everything seems natural. Carefree gardens are places without illusion or artistry, where intervention is kept to a minimum, and where the garden itself looks as though it might almost have evolved on its own. They celebrate the natural progression of the seasons in the growth, flowering and dying back of plants. Plants are indeed a key element – they lead the vision of the garden – while materials and structures are included to harmonize with the plants, to provide climbing frames and supports for them and to make the garden accessible to us. Though an underlying design layout holds things together, evidence of it is eroded wherever possible, appearing only fleetingly in the form of garden features like fences, pergolas, seats and structures made from natural materials that recede beneath the gentle embellishment of unrestrained plants, encouraged to self-seed and to grow into one another.

Lavender, lupins, artichokes and poppies are among a variety of introduced plantings that give informal colourful detail to this relaxed New Zealand garden, amid grasses interspersed with native trees and shrubs. Structures like fences, a table and chairs appear indistinctly through the profusion of naturalistic planting that merges with its surroundings.

A carefree design need not be haphazard. Like all successful designs, its shapes and levels should contain space for both planting and practical areas, such as lawns, for your chosen activities in the garden. Whether in a small urban plot or a large country estate, think of the process as a painting: be bold and generous with your lines and keep things simple, creating large, comfortable shapes wherever possible. There is no point in dreaming up too detailed a scheme because it will soon disappear beneath the planting that follows.

In the absence of order and linear control, the aim of a carefree design is to achieve as natural an appearance as possible. In an open, sunny site, a wildflower meadow would be a suitable alternative to a lawn, for example; it could be cut through with mown paths leading to functional areas (see pages 82–3). Naturalistic fences can be made from hazel hurdles (ready-made woven panels) or from wattle – stakes driven into the ground with flexible willow strips woven through them; both provide a visual screen and a sympathetic boundary. In a rural location, where a solid boundary would prevent you from 'borrowing' the surrounding landscape, an open post and rail fence made from split chestnut will have a low profile and echo the traditional boundaries used for agricultural purposes.

Structures should feel integrated with their surroundings; if made, for example, from reclaimed timber that has already been weathered, they are less likely to stand out. A pergola might be constructed from rustic poles rather than planed timber, and a garden shed may be given a turf or wildflower roof. Other structures can be formed from living plants: an arbour might be created by planting a circle of cherry trees and tying their canopies into one another to make a verdant domed shelter, while fences or trellis made from cuttings of certain types of willow and cornus will sprout and grow. Hedges should include native species in random, natural combinations and will contribute blossom, berries and habitats for insects and animals. Suitable water features could be, say, a wildlife pond or stream that will follow natural contours within the garden. You may decide to create some earthworks to produce contours if you have none. For inspiration, mimic any rivers, lakes or ponds as they occur naturally in the landscape.

Rather than being assembled all at once, a carefree garden is more likely to arise from a gentle process of accumulation as plants, materials and containers are introduced over time. Start with native plant species that will encourage wildlife into the garden. Study your native flora in books of wildflowers or take a walk in the nearest 'wild' place, which could be a park, a building site that has been colonized by wild species, or the local countryside. You can then make informed selections from other plants with a similar 'feel' to what you have already chosen. Don't be seduced by the showy, oversized blooms, colours and leaf shapes of

In my own country garden, cottage-garden plants found their way into beds and containers almost by chance. We planted tall flowering perennials in a random way in the front bed (below) to create a colourful, chaotic display for passers-by. In the vegetable garden (left) herbs and flowers overflow into pots, the surplus simply adding to the pleasure.

modern cultivars. While these may look impressive in isolation, they will stand out in a natural wild garden where indigenous grasses, wild roses, briars, poppies, and woodland shrubs and trees contribute an appropriate sense of naturalness and delicacy.

Using plants that self-seed will ensure that the planting structure alters each year with no further input. What makes a carefree garden so appealing is that changes happen unintentionally and bring with them surprises for the patient gardener as they make their own aesthetic contribution. Watch as your original framework metamorphoses into a different creature year by year. All you need do is step in now and again and perhaps carry out some

The seascape backdrop of an exposed coastal site provides inspiration for a fluid, naturalistic planting. A surprisingly varied selection of drought-tolerant plants such as sage, santolina and phlomis merge together without breaking up the garden's sense of unity.

INTERPRETING CAREFREE STYLE

- Wire fence retained as 'transparent' perimeter
- Use of random planting to link with the landscape
- Beds loosely edged with pebbles
- Old tree trunk and logs used as seating

- Rear fence camouflaged with vigorous climbers
- Existing trees and shrubs absorbed into additional planting: wildflower meadow and beds merge into a composite image
- Placing of furniture looks random and unobtrusive

territorial pruning in order to reshape a living structure or reclaim an overgrown seating area. The challenge is to arrange such gentle delights into a garden where your own intervention is indiscernible from natural growth. This is the reward of a carefree style – a garden you can participate in rather than rule over.

- ◆ Limited palette

- ◆ Inspiration from Eastern philosophy

- ◆ Clean lines

- ◆ No clutter

- ◆ Blocks of colour

Hard surfaces and architectural features – including aluminium containers, glass panels, slatted trellis and timber decking – dominate the scene in this minimal roof garden which I designed for a London client. Elements such as the container-grown plants, sunken beds and a curved seat all relate to one another by sharing similar dimensions, integrating the entire space.

minimal

A minimal garden is a place of studied refinement. The visual impression is created by simplifying the ingredients, so that plants, materials and structural features are set within a pared-down framework of simple proportions that reflects calm, order and balance. Whether the garden is built around bold colours, exotic foliage and distinct textures or more subdued selections, the prevailing sense is one of a carefully considered design approach.

Ideally suited to the urban context, minimal gardens often rely for their effect on hard structures like walls, flooring and containers, assembled in a bold and uncompromising way. This approach can also be seen in the treatment of plants which may be deployed to almost sculptural ends, grouped in blocks of similar species to create 'tonal shapes', or clipped to echo the line of important features. A minimal garden will happily settle around just a few selected plant varieties, making their contribution more powerful as less becomes more.

Minimal implies reduction and, like the Japanese Zen gardens that embody its ideals (see pages 46–7), minimal gardens are designed to induce a state of serenity, even meditation. To this end, you will need either to screen any obtrusive elements such as nearby buildings with clever camouflage or to assimilate them carefully within your design. The quality and enjoyment of a minimal garden lie in

its purity, which must not be compromised, so be selective in the early design stages and resist a temptation simply to fill space. Dramatic tension is created when open spaces are infiltrated with studiously placed plants and objects that provide the garden's focal points. Such elements should draw attention one after another, each absorbing your concentration in turn before the eye moves on.

To strengthen a minimalist design, allow lines and features to become dominant, so that they unify the vision of the garden. A rill of still water might flow into a sunken bed of fountain grass, which in turn runs towards a seat that curves round a corner and along another boundary. If they are built to the same width, all these features will become a single element that unites a large area. Look for horizontal and vertical correspondences like these and avoid disparate, unconnected features. In refusing to clutter and accumulate, the austerity and clean lines of a minimal garden pay homage to what has been selected over what has not. A carefully placed feature or architectural plant will have great impact in a minimal framework as it stands out against the harmony of its surroundings, especially if it is the only feature allowed to govern an area.

Minimal gardens are serene and stylish spaces in which the sheer impact of their purity can be exhilarating. By providing a place in which we can think and relax, a minimal garden can become an almost spiritual location.

The pared-down design of this New Mexico garden is a response to intense climate and striking landscape. Dramatic tension is achieved (left) as a fire pit and its plinth, a focal point within the garden, echo a distant mountain. Balance is key to minimalism and the architecture of the house (below) is impressive enough for only a few selected cacti to achieve a strong visual presence against its adobe walls.

INTERPRETING MINIMAL STYLE

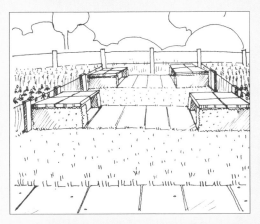

- All previous features except for fence removed
- Bands of sawn stone and strips of lawn create strong repetitive pattern, echoed by block planting in the beds behind
- Seating structures retain clean lines and make an aesthetic contribution well beyond their practical use

- Straight and curved lines delineate features such as wave hedge and shapes of beds
- Wide strips of timber decking match regular rows in the planting
- Seat incorporates straight lines, curves and decking detail

zen

Among the most inspiring images in the history of minimal garden design are the Zen gardens of Japan, some of which are over five hundred years old. Zen is a strand of Buddhism that focuses on the spiritual transformation of an individual through contemplation ('Zen' means meditation). A garden designed along Zen principles is therefore seen as a way of further enhancing a life lived within this philosophy. The aim of Zen gardens is to convey the essence of nature through highly symbolized representations of the world. Their impact endures owing to the beauty and simplicity of their design, their overall clarity and detail giving them a contemporary look even today.

Zen gardens can work on two levels. You may immerse yourself in the philosophy and symbolism they embody to enrich your visual experience of them, or you can accept that they are complex and prefer to look at them uninitiated, absorbing their design and atmosphere instinctively. Whichever way you look at a Zen garden, you can draw from it the inspiration to create a contemporary garden in city or countryside that is rooted in this precise art.

The contents of an authentic Zen garden – be it a tea garden, courtyard or temple garden – are assembled to create an impression of refined natural order. Though in some cases these gardens cover no more than a few square metres, their true sense of scale and proportion is governed by the symbolism of their contents. Rocks, sand, water and plants represent the forces of nature and create a link with the wider physical landscape and, in the patterns of their arrangement, with the landscape of the soul. Pointed rocks depict vast mountains as well as mythical islands that are said to contain the power of immortality. Around these 'islands' swirl raked sand or gravel to symbolize the sea of life, their pure white tones denoting reverence and a sacred space. This sea also alludes to our lives as they unfold before us, the rocks within it representing the obstacles that lie ahead on our journey to spiritual enlightenment.

Water is both a calming and a refreshing presence in the garden. It brings with it the essence of oceans, lagoons, lakes, rivers and marshes. It reflects the sky by day and at night adds depth to the tones of the garden with its dark shadows. Still pools and ponds imply balance and tranquillity, while waterfalls and flowing water introduce soothing movement, gently enlivening the scene with their musical sound and the sparkle of light within their torrents.

Planting in shades of green, with few flowers, conveys the sense of a natural setting. Ornamental maples are ideal for these 'worlds in miniature' as they grow slowly and to moderate size, their delicate feathery foliage creating gentle shadows and adding autumn colour. And bamboo is valued for its evergreen foliage that carries the sound of the ocean whenever the wind passes through its leaves, while cherry and plum trees bring blossom in early spring and symbolize the start of a new year. Everything has a significance, even flowering shrubs like camellias which, because they often drop their flowers in mid-bloom, are thought to symbolize our frailty, reminding us that in the midst of life there is death.

The images show two examples of the balance and harmony inspired by Zen gardens. In the courtyard garden (top), a masterful interweaving of natural and structural elements brings the essence of untamed landscape to the confines of an enclosed space. In the dry gravel garden (right) an understanding of natural order and proportion is represented through the skilful arrangement of stones in a sea of raked gravel.

- ◆ Lush, dense planting

- ◆ Hot, bright colours

- ◆ Dramatic foliage

- ◆ Light and shade

An exotic planting of hostas, grasses, bamboos and many other such devourers of space descends upon timber boardwalks where access looks as though it is soon to disappear. The planting is overpowering, dramatic and predatory, with tall–growing species in the foreground adding to the sense of being right in among the plants.

exotic

Exotic gardens have a bold, magical style characterized by dramatic foliage, intoxicating aromas and large, decadent blooms. They celebrate the exuberance of natural growth and the amazing variety of plants which scramble for a foothold in every scrap of soil beneath the canopies of subtropical forest and jungle alike. Thanks to plant imports, many such subtropical-looking varieties – often far hardier than they would seem – are now widely available in temperate countries, thus opening up the possibility of an exotic garden using foliage plants such as bamboos, hostas, ferns, palms, grasses and phormiums. In exotic style, there is less of the staid 'positional' planting common to, say, a minimal or formal style. The aim is for an overall effect: a profusion of plants growing in close proximity that combine into a dense flora, where the weeds will never stand a chance.

Choosing plants primarily for their foliage creates the ideal backdrop for a mesmerizing choreography of light and shadow as sunlight is reflected, fragmented and filtered by leaves. Structure in this style of garden is present only to enhance the abundance of greenery, by offering a means of support for climbers and trailing plants in the form of trellis, screens and pergolas and, as pathways, permitting access through the wilds of planted zones to hidden seats enshrouded by leaves. Apart from their practical role, seating areas and terraces offer a visual 'breathing space' in contrast to the intense drama and variety of the planting. Paths can be as indistinct as a scattering of shredded bark or log slices placed between plants to help you negotiate your jungle.

Water can provide cool, muted reflections to balance the chaos of massed plants, its sound combining hypnotically with the rustling of leaves in a breeze. A sense of naturalness in the planting will help to further this tranquillity. In the wild, four or five plant species tend to dominate any one area, and in among them will be hidden a further diversity of species. To mimic this, plant

groups of a single species in one spot to give the feel of a coherent environment, then slip in more showy delights. There are so many striking plants that you can create surprises at every turn (see the lists on pages 164–89). Many exotic plants, such as tree ferns, are impressive viewed from above, so why not create raised levels or walkways in your garden? You might include palm-surrounded, shaded pools, decks and connecting boardwalks

through dense foliage. In even the smallest such garden you can become delightfully lost.

Planting should intermingle and be multi-tiered, with tall subjects such as palms, bamboo and even hardy bananas as the canopy, and shade-loving denizens at mid- and lower levels. Allow breaks in the canopy for the sun to illuminate small glades, intensified by the hot colours of exotic flowers like ginger and canna lilies. Let these bright oases become tantalizing destinations in your garden and send fluidly shaped lawns, like green pools, out to greet them. Encourage views to become encircled with foliage by letting climbers dangle from trellis, pergolas and the boughs of trees.

Select all your plants for drama and aim for a variety of leaf shapes, textures and tones in species that will tolerate your coldest temper-atures. Large leaves can be delicate, so you might consider protection by fences or trellis from the damaging effects of strong winds. It is also important to protect vulnerable crowns and stems by mulching and

In a small back garden where space is at a premium, the use of dramatic, exotic plants makes an impact that overrides any sense of spatial deprivation. Here, a lavish, varied collection of architectural and foliage plants – many of which are reasonably hardy – creates intimate seating areas in both sun and shade. Plants such as cordylines, ferns and the fan palm, *Trachycarpus fortunei*, provide shelter (left) and together with the lancewood tree (*Pseudopanax ferox*) and the gigantic leaves of *Rhododendron sinograunde* (above right) turn this small space into a leafy labyrinth.

insulating plants against winter frosts. With their large, thirsty leaves, these plants will favour a moist, fibrous planting compost that is not allowed to dry out.

Consider a design that allows as much space for plants as possible but make sure that practical areas are left sufficiently clear of foliage to be able to use them. Place large trees and shrubs at the front of beds so that you really feel you are in the middle of a jungle. Once you have created an exotic garden, you may find yourself adding incessantly to your leafy domain, so take this into account when you decide the size of such inflexible features as paths and seating areas. The exuberance of your planting can be restrained through the introduction of gentle order and symmetry in the garden layout, and in the siting of key plants and features. But if you want to capitalize on the bounty this style has to offer, leave self-restraint behind and have in mind a stroll in the jungle when you go plant shopping.

INTERPRETING EXOTIC STYLE

- Circular lawn with surrounding stream mimics jungle glade
- Discreet path through plants made of stepping stones or log slices
- Rear fence of bamboo acts as windbreak
- Key plants include banana trees and bamboo

- Garden divided into lawn, natural pool and camouflaged rear seating
- Plants soften boundary between one area and another
- Repetitive use of phormiums adds drama
- Large plants in small gardens give illusion of greater scale

The romantic garden is one of the most sublime of all garden styles. Flower-filled beds with rich combinations of colour and tone, as well as the intoxication of scent, create gentle environments where the hard lines of a design are hidden in the natural abundance of luxuriant planting.

Romantic gardens can take many different forms. In the intimate enclosures of medieval England, covered walks led between beds filled with perennials and herbs to climber-entwined bowers where couples could meet for secret liaisons, hidden within the foliage and flowers of vines, honeysuckle and climbing roses. By the early 1700s, the English landscape movement began to embody a slightly more expansive 'Romantic' approach that helped to free the designs of large-scale gardens from the hold of the formal style. Inspired by the romantic imagery of paintings, this new wave saw the introduction of natural themes into the visual vocabulary of gardens with woodland, water, flowing lawns and rustic-looking buildings. At this time, the desire for an authentic natural vision was such that one designer, William Kent, actually planted dead trees among his living specimens. So the romantic garden began to bridge the gap between the world of art and aesthetics – where decoration is key – and the natural world, with its wilder, more unstructured beauty.

Today, romantic gardens generally exist on a smaller scale than the vast tracts of land familiar to gardeners in the eighteenth century but they embody many of the same ideals. The layout is usually loose and informal, with meandering paths that allow the garden to hold back its secrets, only revealing them on further exploration. There is, nevertheless, a degree of artifice within a romantic garden that sees a decorative requirement placed on all things: while a natural image is sought, it is achieved with cunning. There may, for instance, be a naturalness to the look of deep beds filled with ornamental cottage-garden mixed perennials and annuals, shrub roses and herbs, whose colours intermingle, but such variety in so confined an area is entirely synthetic: the colours, heights and flowering times are all carefully selected. It is the exuberance of the plants that gives these gardens their appeal and the inclusion of unremarkable-looking species and varieties is rare. Owing to the intensity of decorative planting in them, these gardens can require a great deal of maintenance and constant cosseting, so ensure that you will have time enough to care for your creation.

Romantic gardens are filled with scented climbers such as roses, jasmine, honeysuckle and clematis, along with fragrant border plants like lavender, rosemary, lilies, violets, bearded irises, stocks and phlox, grown on or against

Pools of sunlight and dappled shade play across a collection of climbing roses and flowering perennials in this seductive corner. The predominance of pinks and whites in the planting scheme gives the garden an air of refined decoration yet it retains a naturalistic feel through the wealth of lush greenery.

- ◆ Scent

- ◆ Secluded seating

- ◆ Rich in flower

- ◆ Decorative features

romantic

supports such as trellis panels, pergolas, arbours or pyramids. Along with small trees and shrubs like lilac, buddleja, magnolia, apple, plum and pear trees, they help to create a sense of seclusion and intimate enclosure.

Structures, too, have a decorative role to play, although they may be camouflaged with an abundance of plants. But where they show through they should complement the plants; decorative details can be refined or rustic, depending on taste. So a trellis that supports climbing roses might be made from a delicate latticework of timber strips, painted white, green or another suitable background colour, with decorative finials in the shape of points, pyramids or acorns. Or it may be constructed from a rough lattice of round timber poles still covered in bark. Similar approaches could apply to pergolas, picket fences and gazebos.

Paths and hard surfaces should receive a decorative treatment too. Larger areas of stone paving are likely to be broken up with the addition of old bricks, cobbles, gravel and other small-scale materials. Used alone, these small units are well

suited to paths and terraces in a romantic garden as they can easily be arranged into patterns of intimate proportion. Because of their uniform size, bricks can be laid in all manner of rhythmic patterns; basketweave and herringbone work particularly well. If gaps are left, plant aromatic creeping herbs such as thyme and Corsican mint that release their scent when walked on to show nature's infiltration even at ground level. And there can be nothing more romantic than a herb lawn; as long as your soil is not too rich and gets enough sun, you might take up your turf and try a lawn of chamomile, thyme or mint instead.

Adopt a layout with adequate provision for deep beds and plenty of scope for hidden areas and secluded seating, such as benches made of wood or painted metal, perhaps with a curved back and always with enough room for two!

Plan your planting carefully, especially with respect to colour and tone in the garden. Discord or clashing colours could spoil the effect, so consider the ultimate size and shape of plants, their colour and, most importantly, their harmony with the surrounding plants and features. It may help to decide on a gentle colour scheme for the garden first, then look for plants that will help you achieve this. Consider the shade that will be created by larger plants as they grow, to ensure that sun-lovers do not become overshadowed as the garden matures. Then simply sit back in your secluded seat and enjoy your creation.

A journey around the romantic garden shown left becomes a sublime sensory experience. Billowing lavender hedges flank flower-filled borders and a lawn. Rose arches frame vistas as they follow brick pathways to quiet corners, rewarding all who stroll beneath with a delicate perfume.

INTERPRETING ROMANTIC STYLE

- Three arbours provide secluded seating
- Dense rear planting of roses or scented shrubs hides the fence
- Simple layout of herb lawn with brick surround
- Small topiary pieces add decoration

- Pergola entwined with scented climbers conceals central seat and curved topiary spirals
- Brick-paved circle flanked by aromatic plants
- Small pond with bridge separates this part of the garden from other areas

- ◆ Found objects

- ◆ Reclaimed materials

- ◆ An impression of chaos

- ◆ Unsophisticated beauty

As the style of a recycled garden is often led by the available materials, any two areas of the same plot can be very different in feel. A few sections of recycled timber make for a striking seating area (below), their rough simplicity

recycled

complementing the
minimal atmosphere
of this seaside deck.
A collection of shells,
pebbles, stones and
old bricks makes an
intimate paved surface
in another part of the
same garden (right).

There is something very satisfying about finding a use for what others have cast aside and in a 'recycled' garden we are encouraged to look at redundant objects in a new context. Here they interact with planting and other features, buildings and structures, their sense of abandonment and decay enhancing the vitality of living plants. Finding new and unfamiliar uses for discarded items and creating novel combinations makes a striking and often humorous impression with, at times, surprising beauty and almost child-like sensitivity.

A recycled garden can be a stimulating vision, its contents contributing a sense of time past and also telling a story, perhaps that of local industry or geography from which they have been retrieved. In an urban location, for instance, a quick rummage in a builder's skip or a trip to the local rubbish dump can yield old sinks, kettles and baths which, with drainage holes drilled into them, can become planters and containers. Reclaimed bricks and old sections of wrought iron fencing may be used to make walls and barriers that bring instant age to your garden. Railway sleepers, scaffold boards, pallets and other heavy-duty structural elements can be given a new, more delicate role in holding back earth in raised beds filled with vegetables. Even old copper plumbing pipes bent into shapes will make interesting supports into which climbers can entwine.

In a rural area, a ruined barn or farm building might yield old timbers and boards that can be used to construct sheds, decks and summer houses, or be split and made into fences, gates or windbreaks around planted areas. Milk churns, buckets, feeding troughs – even lengths of land drain stood upright – can be used as containers for plants, and pieces of agricultural machinery, like rusty sections of a plough or harrow, are ideal as sculptures in themselves or used as climbing frames for plants.

On the coast, a few beachcombing sessions at low tide can yield lobster pots and fish trays to turn into containers, or old bits of netting to use as trellis and plant supports. Driftwood has a sculptural beauty all its own and can make interesting edging to beds and pathways. Pebbles and crushed shells from the beach retrieved under licence (your local environment agency will advise) make a beautiful random textured surface for

The character of this raised pathway is determined by the random pieces of smooth grey slate assembled as a surface material. With any gaps becoming planting opportunities, the path has a life of its own as it meanders round the side of the house. A balustrade of driftwood pieces flanks the outer edge – more as decoration than protection.

paths and seating areas. When dry they contribute a soft, dusty tone but when wet after rain their myriad true colours and shades are revealed. They can also be formed into mosaic patterns, and larger pebbles will make a decorative edging to beds and pathways. Exemplary among recycled gardens is Derek Jarman's retreat on the English east coast where his adornment of a natural setting through the use of objects he found around him shows extreme sensitivity and beauty.

In a recycled garden anything goes, from the weird and wonderful to the surreal or the bizarre, so the constituents need not be limited to any one source. It's best to forget about an ultimate aesthetic goal and just let the garden evolve. One approach is to start with a collection of found objects and salvage and then play around with different arrangements, placing materials and objects where they seem to fit in, or where the structures they will form might be located. You may, for instance, pile up driftwood against a wall between two vegetable beds where it will be turned into a seat. Large boulders or old tyres that are intended as both sculpture and seating might be placed at the base of a tree. As you introduce these items and begin to arrange them, they will start to dictate a layout by forming new associations between themselves and with the contents and topography of the whole garden.

If just one recycled object – be it street lamp, pallet, tea chest or mannequin – has captured your imagination, place it first, then slowly add in other items as you acquire them, shifting positions as you go. As these recycled items become the theme for your garden, they will start to suggest a vibrant visual layout that also serves to accommodate your planting. The plants may tie in with the structures. For example, rust-coloured heleniums and wallflowers would complement the tones of rusting iron, while prolific climbers and lax-stemmed perennials could clamber over and subdue other structures. On the other hand, the planting may be as eclectic, contrasting and varied as the contents: instead of harmony, try discord, with the acidic, citrus-green foliage of *Euphorbia mellifera* and that of bright hostas emphasizing the rusty tones of old metal, and specific characterful plants introduced as randomly as the recycled objects themselves.

If you are resourceful, plants too can come cheap. Damaged specimens that still have the will to live can be recycled from plant markets and nurseries if you talk to the right person, and bartering with other gardeners is another good source of free plant material. And – very much fitting in with the recycling ethos – planting self-seeding annuals, and propagating and dividing your plants can encourage the garden to, in some sense, recycle itself. Annuals like Californian poppies (see page 188), that contrast their delicate forms perfectly with heavy stone or timber items, will constantly find new locations around the garden and have great effect for only the price of a seed packet. A proliferation of plants already in your possession can also help to populate the garden at no great expense through careful propagation and division (see pages 150–1).

Allow the garden to surprise you and respond to what happens as you make your additions rather than trying to control and predict the outcome. There is always the possibility that you will reach a stage at which you consider the garden finished, then decide to preserve that image. Or the chaos may simply be too much fun, encouraging you to continue with new creations year after year.

- ◆ Vegetables mixed with flowers

- ◆ Ordered beds

- ◆ Crop rotation

- ◆ Edible flowers

- ◆ Companion planting

potager

A medium-sized coastal plot is enclosed for protection from strong biting winds and arranged into a highly functional layout of raised beds. The utilitarian division of space provides for high productivity as every last inch is used for plants, with containers making a valuable contribution. The raised beds make a nutrient-rich planting medium available for hungry plants that would find no sustenance in the sandy, stony soil beneath them.

Other than the spectacle of a garden in full flower, one of the greatest rewards for our labours is that of pulling home-grown produce from the soil and eating it. To many people, however, vegetable plots can seem lonely places of toil where relaxation comes only when all tasks are achieved and the day is over. If such an image clouds your enthusiasm for growing vegetables, but you still cherish a desire for home-grown produce and are prepared to put in the effort, a potager may be the solution.

Potagers, or ornamental vegetable gardens – known in North America and the Antipodes as edible landscapes – have existed for several hundred years in some shape or form. Their recent origins lie mainly in the potagers of France which, since the late sixteenth century, have combined the nation's love of food with an appreciation of ornamental design within gardens. These combination gardens, often set apart as an enclosed area of a larger plot, contain not just

vegetables but also fruit, flowers and herbs. Their constituents date back to early monastic gardens, where a square enclosure with high walls was laid out in a strictly formal manner. In its simplest form, four beds were formed by two crossing paths with a fountain in the centre. Each bed contained a different plant group: vegetables and fruit would feed the brethren, flowers beautify the altar and herbs were used both medicinally and as flavouring for food. This model was reinterpreted on a grand scale in the formally designed gardens of seventeenth-century French chateaux, with breath-taking ornamental arrangements as at Villandry.

A formal design came to govern the potager because of its suitability for a highly productive vegetable garden. It was easy to cultivate rows and small beds with paths between, and geometric shapes allowed maximum use of space. Plants arranged in square and rectangular beds, often edged with lavender, box hedging or herbs like thyme or marjoram, made up the layout. Set within this geometric pattern, seating areas were often at opposite ends of the paths, paved with regular patterns of brick, stone slabs or granite setts.

Formality proved too restrictive for some, and towards the end of the seventeenth century a different type of potager was introduced. This favoured the exuberance and informality characteristic of the romantic style (see pages 52–5). In a romantic potager, the desire for a high yield is tempered by an enjoyment of natural beauty. While the constituents remain the same, the emphasis is on natural and spontaneous planting. The layout is submerged beneath a profusion of plants, lines become hard to distinguish, paths form mazes that conceal secret delights, and fruit trees, vegetables, flowers and herbs are mixed together in beds.

The contents of an informal potager can be quite eclectic, with terracotta pots, old buckets and urns as containers, fences made from reclaimed timber or woven hazel and willow hurdles, and hedges of shrub roses, rosemary or currant bushes. Beds of different sizes might be edged with large pebbles, old drainage pipes, logs or herbs and need not be geometric, while informal paths of broken shells, bark chips or shingle may twist and turn.

Whatever design you settle on, there are a few basic principles and ground rules to bear in mind and the location is all-important. First, you need sunshine: heavy shade will restrict the variety of food plants you can grow and frost pockets will kill off tender young seedlings. The soil should ideally be fertile and free-draining; if it is not, consider raised beds in which the soil is raised 15–30cm/6–12in above the ground and retained by bricks, railway sleepers or timber strips. This helps to improve drainage and means you can import soil to suit the needs of your produce. The width of vegetable beds is traditionally designed to be an adult's reach (about 1.2m/4ft), enabling you to work on your plants without treading on cultivated soil. Make sure you have a water supply and storage for equipment nearby, as well as a place for compost bins, accessible from the garden.

Most vegetables are hungry annual plants that put on tremendous growth in their short but productive lives. Within their different groups they favour certain conditions, so should be planted accordingly, even in an informal garden. The four main groups are legumes (peas and beans), brassicas (like cabbage and broccoli), alliums (onions and garlic) and roots (such as carrots and parsnips). The position of each group changes annually as they rotate around the garden, to stop them exhausting nutrients in the soil and to prevent a build-up of

soil-borne pests. In a standard four-bed crop rotation, legumes fix nitrogen into the soil. They are followed by large-leaved brassicas which consume nitrogen. Brassicas take a lot of nutrients out of the soil so are followed by roots which will split if grown in too rich a soil. Then come the alliums that require fine, well-drained soil to prevent waterlogging (they also rid the soil of carrot root fly). Plant potatoes, tomatoes, globe artichokes, rhubarb and other crops in separate individual designated areas (not rotated).

Fruit trees, if grown, are pruned into cordons (the stems planted at an angle, against a framework of stretched wires for support, with branches pruned into fruiting 'spurs') or espaliers, with tiered branches trained horizontally away from the main stem, often placed against a wall or fence.

In a formal potager, companion flowers such as marigolds and nasturtiums, or flowering herbs like

Whatever layout you choose, a vegetable garden need not be entirely a place of toil and function. Among the uniform rows of vegetables and companion plants in this well-ordered potager, the canes used to provide support are decoratively capped with miniature terracotta forcing bells.

chives, are planted in lines and as low edgings beside the vegetables, while in a naturalistic potager, self-seeded flowers appear randomly among food plants. In either case, they will contribute more than just the beauty of their blooms. The offer of nectar from their open flowers draws in predators like hoverflies, ladybirds and wasps to help combat the destructive presence of aphids, slugs and blackfly. Some, like marigolds, deter pests because of their strong scent; other edible varieties will enhance summer salads. Especially when growing food plants, you should avoid chemical pesticides. Try to accept any losses as part of a natural cycle.

In this vegetable garden what is most important is questionable – the produce or the soaring yellow verbascums and other plants that have been encouraged to infiltrate it. A potager can be as wild as you want it to be, as long as you remember what is edible and what is not.

INTERPRETING POTAGERS

- Hazel woven panels act as windbreak and provide support for espalier fruit trees
- Raised beds made from railway sleepers laid on ground
- Well-organized planting ensures best use of space for productivity

- Organic plot relies on existing trees as cover for useful predators like songbirds and certain insects
- Cost-saving use of reclaimed materials for pathways
- Containerized planting makes use of scarce space
- Larger shade-loving plants placed to the side

♦ Mesmerizing sounds and echoes

♦ Tranquillity with striking reflections

♦ Cool muted tones

♦ Infinite patterns of movement

water

The presence of water in a garden can govern our mood, quietening emotions and soothing the spirit as it draws our gaze with the primeval pull of flames in the dark. In a cool, shaded garden it can accentuate the lush tones of foliage and the reclusive atmosphere of silence. In a hot garden, water presents respite and refreshment from the sun's rays, countering the heat haze with its cool depths. Water brings magical new worlds into a garden: plants rise up through it and live within it, both on its surface and at its margin, imprinting a tapestry of textures on its surface that also tells the story of the weather as it reflects an ever-changing sky.

Water can have many forms in the garden. Small cascades and water steps bring the hypnotic effect of falling water as it performs in the wild, flowing from rivers and over waterfalls. Ponds with non-geometric outlines echo the natural arrival of water in the landscape as it rises from springs and collects as rainfall over impervious rock strata. Wherever water is still, oxygenating pondweed will help to maintain a healthy environment for plants and animals. For a more decorative effect in a small urban garden, water may be pumped gently over pebbles in basins or circulated in wall-mounted features for the refreshing echoes of its rhythmic sound.

A butyl liner laid on soft sand will hold water and help you to achieve whatever shape best suits the garden. Small water features can often be purchased as kits with a pump already installed; all you need to do is connect

Water can become a strong structural feature when, as in this town garden, it is contained in a broad retaining channel that follows the lines of the design. The stillness of its reflections is intensified through the placing of smooth, dark pebbles, giving it an enhanced visual presence that moderates the diverse and colourful elements around it.

The organic shape of this small pond is obscured by a dense marginal planting that helps to hide any structural details – such as liner or brickwork – at its edge. Plants crowd over the water's surface, creating shadows and reflections, while a small deck permits access for gazing into the abyss.

them to a power source (for safety, use a circuit breaker). A simple fountain with a pump in a reservoir can be relatively easy to install but for anything more elaborate you may have to consider employing a specialist contractor, which may involve considerable cost.

Waterways can become design features too. Narrow rills take water on a journey round a garden: they tend to be laid out in geometric patterns, their rectilinear appearance originating in the irrigation channels that brought life-giving water into the early enclosed courtyard gardens of Persia and, later, Spain. Rills can be bold, stark design elements in a modern garden, perhaps linking a succession of square pools sunk into a timber deck or stone floor or running round the boundary of a hot roof garden, bringing its cooling qualities to all

points. They reorganize the free-flowing nature of water and impose order and direction, making the water itself an almost sculptural element. This can be striking in the context of a contemporary design. In a garden designed around natural lines, a stream can be as effective in a less structured manner, echoing the meanders of rivers in the countryside. Unlike the clean lines of a rill, streams should be edged and lined with pebbles and stones to convey a sense of naturalness. Marginal plantings will further soften lines and help to integrate these features in the garden.

Plants associated with water offer a great variety of tones and textures to suit all styles of garden. The gigantic hide-like leaves of *Gunnera manicata* can grow up to 2m/6ft 6in across, in the damp, protective shade at the water's edge, while clumps of *Darmera peltata*, ligularia and hostas add their fleshy leaves to create a verdant lush surround to pool or pond. The sharp blades of flag irises, reeds and rushes cut vertical fine lines that cast elegant reflections on the water's surface. The floating pads of waterlilies and lotus leaves add texture to the water's surface, shading it from the sun and the attention of predatory birds, their flowers displaying exotic beauty as they rise from the water. For a minimal effect, the placing of a single waterlily or clump of reeds can be very effective. If you are combining many different plants in and around your water feature, consider your selection carefully as the introduction of an invasive species can quickly become a destructive presence that is almost impossible to subdue without harming other plants.

Think carefully about the placing of a water feature, especially in a family garden: children must be protected from access to water in gardens, so make features inaccessible by raising

them high above ground level – for example by having a fountain or basin on a tall pedestal – or by fencing them off securely. Alternatively, you could choose a wall-mounted feature or a bubble fountain that presents no possible risk of drowning. In a wildlife pond, however small, ensure that amphibians can crawl out by placing a flat rock or piece of wood half in and half out of the water. To support fish life, a pond should be no shallower than 45cm/18in; in areas that are prone to frost, this can prevent the entire pond from

The bold geometric lines of a raised pool covered with waterlilies mark a strong design detail that contrasts with the seemingly random natural collection of drought-tolerant plants such as sage, thyme, santolina and *Verbena bonariensis*. A raised pool will tend to accentuate the water feature and its contents.

freezing solid. Always avoid placing a pond beneath the overhanging branches of trees and shrubs as the fallen leaves will rot beneath the water and cause nutrient imbalance that will be detrimental to plants and creatures.

- Drought-tolerant plants

- Dramatic shapes

- Silver-grey foliage

- Sun-bleached background tones

Moisture-storing cacti, succulents and plants with slender pointed leaves, all adept at dealing with hours of withering heat, characterize this dramatic dry garden. The structure is formed entirely through architectural planting that makes a striking picture which is anything but sparse. There is an array of similar-looking plants that can create an impressive spectacle even in gardens where conditions may not be quite so arid as this.

dry

Gardens in dry locations have a sun-bleached intensity. The plants have to work hard for nourishment in soil that is usually free-draining and low in nutrients while the sun's powerful rays often override all other considerations. Xeriscape – or 'water-smart' gardening – is a horticultural movement originating in North America that offers a stylish solution to the problems of gardening in areas of low rainfall. The idea is to work with, rather than against, the resulting conditions and seek out drought-tolerant plants. A strong yet naturalistic style emerges, where plants and materials are inspired by, and linked to, the surrounding landscape and local climate. These gardens may even have no visible boundary to separate them from the surrounding landscape.

Materials like stone, brick, adobe and wood may be used for structures and surfaces and will lend unobtrusive tones to a dry garden. The intensity of the heat is often mirrored in the gardens themselves where hot, dry conditions and starved soil distil the aroma of plants like artemisias, juniper, clary sage, thyme and catmint to almost narcotic strengths. Foliage is typically small and narrow in shape, to reduce water loss, or succulent and moisture-retaining, with silver, grey and dusty green tones that reflect sunlight and merge with patterns within the landscape. Flowers have their own unique intensity to attract pollinators, with bright yellows, sharp blues, burning reds and pure white appearing like jewels in an allusion to the rich mineral deposits that lurk beneath the barren ground in which they grow.

Native plants, arranged in random groupings, will be best suited to your location and conditions, so you need to investigate what is on offer. In many countries an internet service will provide lists of plants native to an area – all you require is a postal

or zip code. However, xeriscape gardening need not be restrictive and the introduction of adaptable plants from similar climates elsewhere in the world will allow for more scope in design. Such a garden will require little in terms of cosseting and maintenance, perhaps only a gravel mulch to fill in between developing plants. For some dry gardeners, even weeds may be a welcome addition.

Gardens that grow out of dry conditions can be both striking and simple, however. Some desert gardens almost have the quality of a lunar landscape. Thick, dusty walls of adobe, rammed earth or clay brick that insulate against the sun's heat, with small windows to preserve shade inside buildings, take on the muted tones of plants. Pathways can be no more than caked dirt tracks between beds, with perhaps a strip of pebbles along their border as demarcation. Dry gardens are

often just carefully managed expanses of native plants, embellished with a few sympathetic plant imports and subtle decorations on the ground or the walls. Boundaries may be only token, such as cactus hedges or flimsy fences of timber palings. In this way desert gardens will merge easily with the landscape around them and remain unobtrusive.

On the other hand, these gardens can be more elaborate. To enhance the silvery tones of a dry garden, include sculptures and use brightly coloured hard materials adorned with mosaic tiles, pathways made from terracotta tiles or mosaic fragments, and colourful perennial and annual plants that make the space feel more like a garden. In the sun's brightness the pigmentation of strong colours on walls and buildings is enhanced and sharpened against a backdrop of clear blue skies.

In this desert garden, designed by Steve Martino, structures and plants create dramatic shadows and sharp lines. Round posts and tall painted columns join spiky blue-grey agaves in a sculptural grouping that rises from a soft, natural underplanting. With crisp, bright light, strong shadows and clear blue skies, gardens in sunny locations can achieve beauty and impact through a relatively simple design.

Bright colours serve to accentuate the muted tones of drought-tolerant plants whose foliage can look as though it has had the life washed out of it.

Whatever drama and impact desert and dry-garden plants may lose in their leaf colour, they make up for in shape and size. Many are very exotic-looking and have an almost alien appeal, such as golden barrel cacti, prickly pear and cactus forms of euphorbia, together with succulent agaves, aeoniums and aloes, perennial yuccas, echiums and coneflowers, palms and trees like tamarix, eucalyptus and pinon pine. For plant groupings using these natives of Africa, America, Australia and the Mediterranean, heat is not a problem (though they will also thrive in less extreme conditions), but any moisture retention within the soil, or a sharp decline of temperature overnight, may cause difficulties.

In all dry gardens shade is essential for those who inhabit and work in them. Buildings often have covered verandahs that look out over the garden so that it may be enjoyed even in the midday sun. Trees and palms create shade for seating areas and for plants with a low sun threshold. Less permanent shade can be provided by a canvas awning stretched over four upright poles guyed into the ground. For shade directly overhead, screening with slatted timbers or netting will create some respite from the sun's rays and an enclosure of timber posts or stakes will allow a breeze to pass through while breaking the full force of the drying winds that would otherwise damage and burn more tender foliage.

Though you may be dealing with a palette of dramatic and architectural-looking plants in areas where there is intense exposure to heat, this need not prevent you from achieving refinement in your planting. In another area of the garden featured left, cacti stand beautifully erect, crowning a subtle arrangement of tones and textures that would be at home in a traditional herbaceous border. Even in harsh conditions, with sensitivity you can evoke a balance and naturalness through sympathetic planting.

Mediterranean

The dry gardens of the Mediteranean have a sun-baked, evocative style in which romanticism merges effortlessly with formality. Muted tones combine with the scent from flowers and foliage and the gentle order of clipped shapes to create a sense of refined naturalness and tranquillity. Through the long days of summer, plants and features are drenched in sunlight that casts stark, graphic shadows, forming a backdrop that invests these gardens with a seductive, intense atmosphere. Though unique to the area, this style can be imitated wherever hot, dry conditions prevail.

Cypress trees are a favourite identifying feature of these gardens. Clipped into screens, pencil-like columns or structural blocks, they denote the garden's boundaries and inner dimensions. Their

dark shapes become visual anchors for other less formal elements, like the twisted silver stems of figs with their palmate leaves, or the lacework canopies and gnarled trunks of olive trees.

Rendered or dry stone walls, with terraces of terracotta tiles or hand-made bricks, absorb heat during the day, then radiate it into beds of iris, lavender, rosemary, roses and herbs to release their scent at night. The rough texture and detail of the landscaping materials is tempered by the precision of the plants' tight, narrow leaves and their delicate and exotic blooms, each enhancing the qualities of the other.

Terraces with pools of water shelter in the shade of pergolas that drip with vines, jasmine and wisteria. On patios that bake in the sunshine, terracotta and stone pots of citrus trees, oleander, myrtle, clipped evergreen magnolias and bay trees mark out functional areas with style. Lawns, prone to drying out in the heat of high summer, are usually kept small. A herb lawn is often a preferred solution in the free-draining soil that gives rise to these dry, aromatic gardens.

Wherever possible, scented plants are included. Herbs scramble up walls and along pathways, seeding themselves in cracks and soil pockets that provide the minimal nutrients they require. Low hedges are formed from hyssop, dwarf lavender or clipped box, while larger lavenders, rosemary and clipped bay are often chosen for taller hedges.

The robust and luxuriant planting of the garden featured above and left presents a bold assembly of shapes, tones and textures. Balance and good proportion are enhanced as sun and shade focus attention on structural features such as columnar cypress trees, walls, pots of agapanthus and clipped shrubs such as box. Within this framework more fluid elements such as climbers, flowering shrubs and perennials clothe the structural bones of the garden and add a lighter touch to the space as a whole.

Plants sometimes receive a formal, sculptural treatment; for instance, an avenue of olive or bay trees, running either side of a small path or the approach to a house, might be trained into lollipop-shaped half-standards, or a succession of large rosemary bushes may be clipped into cubes to contrast with the lax growth of herbs planted around them. Simple devices like these reflect the engaging combination of naturalness and stylish intervention that characterizes Mediterranean gardens.

◆ Combination of distinct styles

◆ Variety of colour and texture

◆ Diverse sources of inspiration

◆ Gardens beyond boundaries

fusion

A clear meeting of styles is evident in this garden where strong formal lines predominate in the use of clipped evergreen hedges and topiary shapes. With the water channel (below), these lay down an ordered profile within the garden that is seen all year. This formality is infiltrated by a loose, carefree planting that

flourishes and recedes annually, reflecting the seasons. The combination of styles creates an exciting garden where each intensifies the experience of the other.

Garden styles often bring with them a set of rules as to the sort of contents, layout and approach that are appropriate. These may seem narrow and intimidating to a new gardener and can squeeze out any potential for individual expression. A fusion garden does not exercise such constraints and this allows us to do exactly as we like. Feel free to break the rules – but remember that fusion is not an excuse simply to rehash and throw together: it is a method that uses rich and diverse sources, and is the result of careful thought and consideration. Whether the integration of styles is partial or total, the gardens that arise will often cross the defining lines of their sources and be characterized by an interweaving of recognizable themes.

If a multitude of design ideas confuses you as you try to settle on just one genre for your garden, then fusion is an opportunity to capitalize on your eclectic tastes. As you gaze at different images of your favourite gardens, seek out the features you find most appealing and establish what it is that you particularly like. Then look for new connections between them as you try to assemble these various elements into just one garden. Fusion gardens show how you can mix styles in a harmonious way, as in the images shown here. If, for example, you like the symmetry of formal style, you can make this the basis for your design but plan a romantic or carefree planting scheme that will eventually obscure the geometry.

Introduce your ideas one by one and link them together. Timber raised beds, for example, may give you the element of control and order that you like in a small town garden, while a terrace of warm terracotta tiles laid in geometric patterns will bring a minimal effect to a functional space. The architectural and structural plantings that catch your eye as you wander round garden centres and nurseries will create drama and movement when added to the beds contained within the minimal formality of such a garden's framework.

A fusion garden may clearly show the sources of influence as, for example, in the case of a Japanese garden that has been given a Western interpretation. Here the arrangement of rocks and structures might seem true to its origins but an infiltration of other influences may be visible in, say, the use of cacti or other unfamiliar gaudy plantings and modern furniture. The sources of fusion gardens can, on the other hand, become almost completely obscured as they are overpowered by the new composite image created. This is typical of gardens that combine native plants from different countries as well as incorporating a variety of materials and influences from many sources.

Although there are no rules for a fusion garden, there is one important consideration. Compromise can be your worst enemy, so it is essential that you have a firm grasp of the styles you wish to combine and commit yourself to breaking them up and re-working them convincingly. If you are tentative, what you achieve will lack the bold excitement of gardens created through breaking boundaries. As your plan begins to take shape – and your confidence grows with it – you can increase the number and variety of inclusions. Fusion can be what you want it to be: the field is yours to play and experiment.

The original inspirations of a design can become so interwoven that they merge into a garden that goes beyond the boundaries of stylistic interpretation. In this dynamic and eclectic garden (left), varied plants, materials, textures and ornament unite in a truly individual composition.

INTERPRETING FUSION STYLE

- Romantic planting of scented and aromatic flowering plants softens the lines of a formal framework
- Side seats beneath rose arches and rear seat beneath small trees create intimacy
- Trees and shrubs interspersed with perennials form a dense, layered planting

- A minimal take on a formal design
- Plants selected for suitability to clipping and shaping
- Dominant circular pattern of plant on rear fence echoed in paving detail on lawn governs design

With an idea of a suitable style for your garden and a fair understanding of the conditions of your plot, you should now be ready to assemble a selection of features and details that will make the vision real. Some of these will inevitably be functional elements like fences and paved areas, while others will be more decorative, such as trellis, containers or a water feature. Whatever items you opt for, they will probably be available in an array of styles and made from a wide variety of materials. As the appearance of any of these features can greatly affect the look of your garden, make sure that what you select feels at home in your design.

For instance, in a formal garden containers will be sophisticated rather than rustic and symmetrically placed in pairs or rows, their style repeated throughout the garden. Hedges are likely to be clipped into uniform shapes and furniture with clean, geometric lines may become a strong design feature in itself. In a carefree garden, on the other hand, containers are likely to be weathered and randomly placed, hedges to be grown from mixed plants left to develop loosely and furniture to be rustic and natural in appearance. In this way, each element selected will be in keeping with the garden's character, strengthening the design that inspired it and giving the garden an overall unity as well as making it comfortable to use and pleasant to look at.

To help with your selection, I have assembled a 'scrapbook' of elements, covering a wide range of features, and in this chapter I consider their suitability to particular styles of garden. I have grouped them together into three categories: natural elements, covering living and growing plant ingredients like grass and hedges, as well as water; garden architecture, which includes walls, fences and all kinds of paving; and decoration – the all-important detailing found in garden furniture, sculpture, plant supports and even lighting.

assembling the elements

natural elements

Lawns and meadows

A great deal of thought and energy goes into devising the 'look' of a garden and into detailing both ornament and plantings – yet the lawn, frequently the most used area, often receives little of this creative attention. As a growing element, a lawn presents a visual breathing space amid the diversity of other garden areas and features. In many senses, it is the ultimate functional area – there is nothing to rival lying back on a fresh green carpet in spring and no better sight than a freshly mown lawn on a summer's day. (For more details on making a lawn from seed or turf, see pages 132–3). Lawns have become a representation of our control over nature but they can also be more than the restful strip of greenery that is mown regularly to within an inch of its life in the pursuit of perfection.

With a little inventiveness and a bag of seed, you can transform an area earmarked for a lawn. Wildflower meadows are a natural phenomenon wherever grass still grows in the wild and one which is especially suited to a carefree style of garden. Where a lawn need not be entirely utilitarian, the green carpet, so lush and vibrant in spring can bring further delights as it releases colourful secrets in summer. Wildflowers, sown within a balanced grass seed mix, will make a lawn an area to rival the most elaborate herbaceous border. It is important to use a mix suited to your local flora or you risk importing invasive and rampant species. A colourful lawn need not be restricted to the summer months: the addition of bulbs such as crocuses, daffodils and snake's-head fritillaries brings pleasure in spring, while colchicums and cyclamen brighten the shortening days of autumn. Bulbs have to be planted individually, using a planter or dibber. Converting an existing lawn is quite a complex process that usually involves removing existing grass and reducing the soil's fertility so that delicate wildflowers are not swamped by lawn grasses and tough weeds. A local supplier should advise you on appropriate bulbs and seed for your climate and soil conditions.

1 Meadow flowers bring a natural beauty and pattern to our sometimes over-managed strips of lawn. Here, summer flowers – cornflowers, corncockles, ox-eye daisies and corn chamomile among them – provide a rich, varied and colourful carpet that contrasts with the weathered timber of the house and boardwalk.

2 Lawns can become almost sculptural in their effect. Here, in an elegant pattern that mixes curves with sharp lines, a box-edged grass terrace provides the garden with a geometric green motif. Formal in design and perfect in proportion, this lawn contributes a sense of calm and order.

'The green carpet, so lush and vibrant in spring can bring further delights as it releases colourful secrets in summer'

3 A contemporary planting shows unusual combinations, with annual flowers such as marigolds and nicotiana interspersed with barley and perennial *Verbena bonariensis* among the grasses. This gives a rich, textural effect, further embellished by shell-topped canes that mark a pathway linking this area of the garden to a separate, more structured garden lying beyond the woven willow fence.

4 A dense grassy meadow strewn with bright yellow buttercups makes a deep and lush lawn alternative in this large, open garden. Signs of human intervention are kept to a minimum, with only a narrow mown pathway leading to a secluded seat.

Earth

Soil need not be consigned to flower beds and borders, with the sole task of providing for your plants' needs. It can be used to make outoor turf seats and even find its way on to roofs, offering green grass and a profusion of flowers as an uncharacteristic skyline. It is a versatile medium that has been appreciated since times past when it was banked and made into mounds, both as a means of protection around dwellings and as a focus of worship at sacred sites. Taking inspiration from such practical and symbolic use of soil invites a sculptural treatment in your own garden. Decorating the bare earth itself can be dramatic. You can also evoke powerful, even mystical associations by constructing earth mazes and other graphic forms on the ground, while a bank of soil can raise planting to new heights and add depth to even the smallest of gardens. So look to the contours of your plot and seek to create some earthbound drama.

Patterns may be made in a grassed area by building mounded contours or by digging out shallow trenches and back-filling them with sand, pebbles, chalk or other contrasting material. You might build a network of low, raised features by banking soil into sinuously curved forms - this can have an unexpected, artful effect as part of an otherwise ordinary lawn. When planted with low hedges of box or aromatic herbs, these trenches or mounded contours can make gentle geometric mazes in a minimal design or loose, aromatic divisions in a potager or a romantic garden.

A perplexing pattern of trenches or mounds – either planted up to give a sense of change, or filled with sand or pebbles for a more permanent, unchanging appearance – can be created around features and functional areas to suit the strange perspectives and proportions of a conceptual or fantasy garden. More simply, in the longer grass or wildflower meadow of a carefree or exotic garden you might adjust the height of the mower blades to fashion a low maze or pattern by contrasting the texture of long and short.

1 A mesmerizing labyrinth illuminated with tiny candles is a striking and unexpected image at ground level. Such a feature, cut into existing grass, can be created in any garden.

2 Because soil is malleable it can be worked into sculptural shapes such as hummocks and mounds or other patterns. Disguised with a sprinkling of grass seed, this crocodile lies silently in wait for its prey.

'Soil is a versatile medium that has been appreciated since times past. A bank of soil can raise planting to new heights and add depth to even the smallest of gardens. So look to the contours of your plot and seek to create some earthbound drama'

3 With a waterproof layer covered by a planting medium – often a sandwich of topsoil and drainage material – a roof can become a living part of your landscape. Sedums and sempervivums, both suitably drought-tolerant, have here colonized an old shed.

4 Formed simply of natural stone blocks placed on bare earth, this spiral creates a dynamic and mystical pattern that can be walked into and out of at the same time.

Hedges and topiary

Hedges delineate boundaries and mark out divisions – but they have an added potential. As they comprise living, growing material, hedges may, through tight clipping, be sculpted into structural elements in a garden. They can be made into mazes and patterned parterres for formal gardens and structured potagers; the most suitable plants are slow-growing evergreens like yew, for taller features, and box for low hedges. When grown from a mixture of native species and allowed to assume loose, natural forms, hedges become the gentle enclosure to a carefree haven and provide valuable wildlife habitats. Formed from deciduous plants like hazel, hawthorn and roses, or from herbs like lavender, hedges can be used to create strange structures in a recycled garden or make decorative demarcation in a romantic design.

Clipped into tightly controlled shapes, hedges may be used to mark out important lines within a design. With their shape they can echo other features, such as patterns in brickwork or the repetitive layout of narrow, staggered terraces or raised beds. With hedges clipped into the shape of crenellated walls, anyone's home can become their castle, hedges thus becoming part of a fantasy landscape. Perforated with arches or windows, they offer views out or allow glimpses into other areas, creating an air of anticipation and revelation as you move about the garden. Essential to many styles, hedges will screen unsightly objects in the surrounding landcape or compartmentalize a garden, making it seem varied and larger than its actual dimensions.

An extension of clipped hedging, topiary stands on its own as living sculpture, providing a focus and a visual anchor to the more chaotic and exuberant plantings of herbaceous borders. Usually formed from evergreen plants, topiary is relied on in formal designs for a sense of poise and dignity. It also has an atmospheric presence that can be moulded into strange, contorted profiles for a fantasy landscape. Clipped into large, rolling globes, elegant spirals or more enigmatic shapes, it takes on a dramatic, even humorous, romantic role. A surreal gathering of shapes can be assumed by topiary pieces for an unmoving game of chess, or a procession of random geometric shapes in a conceptual garden.

1 Topiary pieces can become striking features in a garden – particularly when trained over the years to the size and volume of this trio of square-based yew pyramids. With a permanent evergreen structure they have great architectural presence. In summer their form is emphasized by sun and shade and in winter it can support the magical tones of fallen snow or heavy frost.

'Clipped into tightly controlled shapes, hedges may be used to mark out important lines within a design'

2 A garden is cleverly divided up by pathways bordered by radiating beech hedges. Some of the hedging plants them—selves have been allowed to grow into small trees to provide a loose, leafy canopy that softens the linear layout.

3 In a garden of different levels, low topiary pieces are juxtaposed with hard land-scaping. A flight of stone steps is visually continued in

a block of clipped yew at its summit, with other pieces clustering around a wall and making a soft edging to a lawn. Echoing structural shapes in stone and planting creates a stimulating interplay of shapes and textures.

4 A collision of clipped hedges makes a dramatic focus to this garden entrance. The wave–like shapes have a rhythmic precision and a

strong sculptural presence that greatly exceeds the usual expectations of a hedge.

5 Like a huge, convoluted caterpillar, this old hedge of *Lonicera nitida* has outlived its restraints and is now clipped to more natural dimensions. Such an effect can be achieved by either tending to an old hedge that has begun to topple, cutting into a mature, regimented hedge to encourage curves, or planting and training one from scratch.

Water: pools, rills and fountains

There are many ways to bring water into a garden. Still pools and ponds hold fathomless depths, mirrored reflections and delicate ripples that mark the passing of a breeze. Touched by a leaf from a nearby plant, the confined world of a garden and the infinite, mystical qualities of water are bridged. Moving water enlivens the dullest of corners, with cascades, fountains and streams creating rhythmic sounds that make an elemental link with the wilds of nature. A range of plants and creatures thrive within water and at its edge, turning ponds into a world in miniature within your garden.

A water feature can be a dominant element in a garden – such that it leads the design – or it may be something that merges naturally within an assembly of plants and other features. Whatever its ultimate appearance, a pool will need a waterproof lining and, where the water is to be kept moving, a pump and a reservoir; this equipment can be purchased through small ads in the back of gardening magazines or from larger garden centres. It is worth thinking about the method of construction you will use and how it can be made to blend with the overall design (see also Water gardens, pages 66–9).

Fountains that issue jets of water often take a sculptural form. Made from brickwork, tiles or clad in smooth timber to geometric or uniform dimensions, they will suit a formal or minimal interpretation. A modern look can be achieved with a feature made from metal, glass or sawn stone. But formed from twisted copper piping, bamboo canes or a pile of rocks with holes drilled through them – or indeed using any natural element that might house the nozzle of a jet – they will be better suited to the quirky style of a recycled garden or the more natural appeal of a carefree one.

For dramatic effect, features such as fountains and rills can be inter-connected so that they make dynamic lines that flow around a garden, or they may stand alone as focal points where the presence of water will act as a counterpoint to the surrounding garden. By camouflaging features through building them at low levels from natural stone and surrounding them with marginal plants, water can play a more sublime role, contributing no more than a gentle bubbling sound.

1 This still pond creates a mirror for its surroundings. Deep green reflections and the darker shadows of nearby trees, fragmented with glimpses of a clear blue sky, accentuate the tone of the brighter green floating plants and marginals at its edge. Wooden decks have an affinity with water and seats allow participation in a scene of restful intensity.

2 A succession of galvanized buckets makes a whimsical cascade atop a gently sloping wall. Though this water feature looks extensive, it would be comparatively easy and inexpensive to mimic, requiring a row of buckets with nozzles and a reservoir below them containing a pump to send water back up to the first receptacle.

3 Against a bright tiled wall an individual fountain of reptilian heads gushes water into a pool below. If you can guarantee a free flow of water, anything can be the inspiration for such a striking feature.

'Moving water enlivens the dullest of corners, with cascades, fountains and streams creating rhythmic sounds'

4 Intensified through contrast with a varied naturalistic planting, this raised slender rill, or channel of water, makes an eye-catching focal element in a dry garden. Thirsty plants crowd forward as if seeking refreshment, like parched animals at a water trough.

5 In the smallest of gardens, the audible and visible qualities of water are readily appreciated. Here, a submerged pump in a simple but elegant square container enlivens the water surface with gentle movement and soothing sounds.

Water: swimming pools and hot tubs

A swimming pool can play an important part in a garden as a decorative water feature if it is considered as a design element. If you are planning one, collaborate with your pool designer or supplier and, where possible, use similar construction materials to help integrate it with other elements of your garden such as terraces or garden buildings. Alternatively, you can use camouflage and disguise to create a clever illusion: weir-edged pools, in coastal locations, can seem almost to merge with the sea, bringing the ocean's vastness into the garden as the lack of a visible border at the water's edge tricks the eye. A curved outline and a variety of lush, large-leaved plants in proximity to its edge can make a swimming pool appear more natural. Hot tubs – another desirable outdoor pleasure, where budget and climate permit – have less aesthetic potential but are still worth treating as creatively as possible.

Siting is crucial, especially if the pool or hot tub is to become a focus in the garden. In practical terms, swimming pools are best sited in a sunny location away from deciduous trees whose falling leaves might be a nuisance. A pool's shape need not be rectangular but can take on an exciting curvaceous profile to echo the organic shape of beds or local land formations. And the arrangement of poolside furniture and planted containers should correspond with other areas within the garden to help in its integration.

With a little imagination, hot tubs can become at least a sympathetic feature in a garden layout. A decking surround looks good as well as being highly practical: decks may be created on different levels with a variety of seating combinations, and a wooden lid over the tub will keep it concealed when not in use. Otherwise a hot tub should be a discreet inclusion that makes little impact, perhaps concealed among large boulders and evergreen trees and shrubs to give the appearance of a natural hot spring. When looking at potential sites, always contemplate the views from inside your pool or tub so that you make the most of any landscape that may be visually borrowed.

Hot tubs, and especially swimming pools, can be costly to install, and the running costs are considerable, though for many these factors are outweighed by the active pleasures these features bring to a garden.

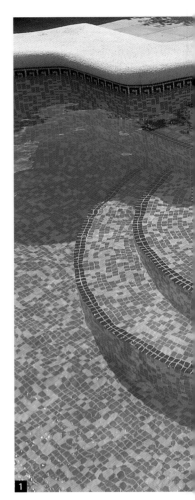

1 When outline, proportion and materials undergo artistic interpretation, a pool can be transformed into a striking visual element of the garden. Here, the clever design of circular steps combines a random flickering pattern of bright mosaic tiles with the generous smooth contours of the pool's moulded stone edge to great sculptural effect.

2 Rather than being tucked away in a corner, the swimming pool has been boldly placed at the centre of this New Zealand garden. A decorative use of materials in the treatment of the pool and its surround, with a sympathetic exotic planting, turns the swimming pool into a positive element that merits its focal position.

3 The view across the river from this high-rise hot tub should be enough to rival the pleasures of sitting in it. With a user-friendly decking surround and a bold circular design, the hot tub is a well-integrated feature that greatly contributes to the overall appeal of this inner-city balcony garden as well as being entirely private.

'Swimming pools and hot tubs are essential outdoor pleasures where space, budget and climate permit and should be treated as creatively as possible to integrate them into the garden'

garden architecture

Man-made boundaries

A wall or fence is often thought of as merely a boundary marker, security screen or windbreak and therefore receives little creative attention. Thus all too often an uninspiring boundary fence, for example, lets down an otherwise successful garden design. If considered as an aesthetic backdrop, a wall or fence can make an effective contribution as a visual framework for your plants and other features. As well as performing its functional role, it will also screen the garden from any unwelcome views or features that surround it.

The role of boundaries as a major design element is most obvious in minimal and formal gardens, where walls of smooth render or glass bricks, or trellis made from slatted hardwood timber, strips of metal or intricately woven bamboo, are kept clean and clear of plants. On the other hand in exotic, carefree and other informal styles of garden, a wall made from adobe, dry stone or reclaimed bricks, or a fence made from hazel hurdles, split chestnut posts or recycled timber will, as the garden matures, be embellished with shrubs and climbers. Boundaries thus become mere glimpses of a structural layout that draws together plants and other elements, containing the vision as a whole by the gentlest of means.

The average wall or fence is less than 20cm/8in wide and can raise a boundary or screen up to 1.8m/6ft high, which makes it an effective method of demarcation. This economy of space, when compared to the width of a hedge, for example, is of particular benefit to smaller plots. Built to last from brick, stone, metal, treated timber or wood that naturally withstands weather, man-made boundaries display constancy and bring architecture out among the plants. Walls can always be painted to create a colourful backdrop and fences may be constructed with a decorative pattern.

Building a wall can be a specialist task as it may need proper footings and, especially if tall, the skills of a bricklayer or stonemason. Because of the weight of supported plants as well as buffeting by the prevailing wind, fences should be securely anchored between posts that are firmly bedded in the ground, possibly even in concrete. Any panels should ideally stand 5cm/2in above soil level, to prevent the timber absorbing moisture and rotting.

1 Lengths of hazel and willow are woven together to make a naturalistic feature that should last for up to fifteen years before decay starts to become a problem. Separating a lawn from a more enclosed garden area with its undulating horizontal lines, this style of fence suits a relatively carefree planting.

3 Even the most conventional of designs can be given a contemporary twist. The outline and proportions of this boundary 'fence' give a traditional impression but closer examination reveals the materials to be sheets of galvanized steel overlaid with grey-painted trellis.

4 Birds, dragonflies and other small winged creatures make a colourful relief on this bright wall and replace any overbearing sense of containment with a lively and imaginative appearance.

2 A curved rendered wall painted in warm terracotta comes to life with the effects of sunlight and shadow playing across it. Leaving functionality aside, this feature makes a great contribution to the garden as a foil for the architectural profile of the cacti that stand in front of it.

5 In this wild and carefree garden a fence becomes an almost invisible feature with a few lengths of wire stretched between short posts, allowing enjoyment of the view and the natural planting that is extended well beyond the garden's boundaries.

'Built to last from brick, stone, metal, treated timber or wood that withstands weather, man-made boundaries display a constancy in the garden and bring architecture out among the plants'

Paved surfaces

Paths and paved areas make a garden accessible and usable. They map out utilitarian areas such as terraces and lawns and separate them from zones reserved solely for flowering plants, like beds, borders and wildflower meadows. Paths lead us through gardens: they will slow us down if they meander or encourage us on if they run in a straight line. Decorative features such as seats and sculpture recede visually when sited at the end of a long, straight path. Pathways can also be designed to make us stop and admire a feature or pause to contemplate the garden on a seat positioned at a junction or turning point. Providing an even, stable surface, these areas indicate to us where it is safe to walk without risk of damaging plants. Terraces and patios are extensions of living areas; in offering hard standing for chairs and tables, they become arenas for activities such as dining, socializing or simply lounging.

The style of path or seating area will be largely dictated by the materials you choose; they can harmonize with nearby plant foliage or make a stark contrast to it, adding to the visual impact of the garden. Using reclaimed bricks or stone slabs will create an air of instant maturity, while loose gravel or cobbles bedded in mortar makes for an informal surface (though this can still be set within precise formal dimensions). Small units such as bricks, granite setts and terracotta tiles allow intricate, repetitive patterns to create a decorative surface. In a carefree or exotic garden paths may comprise no more than a sprinkling of bark or broken shells, whereas in contemporary gardens 'paved' areas can be made from coloured concrete, glass bricks or rubber matting.

Terraces should be built with a gentle fall, so that rainwater can run off. For a lasting, even surface of, say, stone slabs or brick, you will need a sub-base of compacted hardcore or poured concrete. Some expensive paving materials such as York stone, terracotta tiles or granite setts may require a specialist contractor, so bear this in mind before getting carried away with potentially costly elements in your design. Always try out any areas that you will commit to hard landscaping before work goes ahead. Take chairs and tables out into the garden and see how the proposed site feels. Consider the views from a seating area and observe how the furniture looks when seen from elsewhere.

1 Small units of regular dimensions such as brick can be arranged into repetitive patterns to suit your design. Here a charming terrace of reclaimed red bricks holds back an exuberant planting to define a seating area and make space for pots. Bricks laid in a basketweave pattern create a decorative appearance. Small areas are often laid on sand and cement over a layer of crushed hardcore.

3

'The style of path or seating area will be largely dictated by the materials you choose; they can harmonize with nearby plant foliage or make a stark contrast to it, adding to the visual impact of the garden'

2 Loose materials such as cobbles, pebbles, gravel and sand can be arranged into random patterns in gardens of any style – provided they are laid on a level base with a weedproof membrane beneath them to prevent plants growing through. Here, swirling lines of blue-grey gravel and pale, smaller-scale grit have been carefully rolled and segregated by slim metal bands to form an unusual organic pattern that befits the central wooden sculpture.

3 The pale dusty tones of stone slabs offer a perfect foil to the fresh green colours of massed agapanthus leaves and their blue-topped architectural flower stems. The geometric precision of this paving layout has an immaculate minimalist appearance that is both stylish and serene.

Decks and decking

Timber decking offers a stylish alternative to dusty or muddy lawns the world over. Descendant of the porches and verandahs of ancient Japanese dwellings, decks bring lighter tones to dark, shaded gardens where grass will never grow well. They are easy to keep clean, by scrubbing or washing with a pressure hose every now and then, and offer a warm, textured surface. A timber deck is a relatively safe flooring for children as it often comes with non-slip grooves and provides a softer, less abrasive surface than brick or stone, making any falls less painful. The directional lines of their timbers can make a garden appear wider or longer, depending on which way they run.

A treated softwood deck can be painted or stained and a 'sustainably harvested' hardwood deck will retain its rich, natural colours for some time if the timbers are oiled. On the other hand both soft and hardwoods are often allowed to bleach in sunlight to a silvery grey tone. As they are considerably less heavy than stone, decks are a practical solution for the flooring of roof gardens. They may also be raised on stilts above an exotic garden or over water, with connecting boardwalks to give aerial views of the plants and garden below. In a modern, minimal garden a deck might be made of metal – more for its visual impact than as a barefoot experience! In a recycled garden, a reclaimed oak floor might be used as an outdoor feature.

Always raise a wooden deck above the ground to prevent moisture being absorbed into the timbers. This is normally done using tanalized timber joists raised on one or two bricks above a 30cm/12in concrete foundation. On a roof terrace, the joists should be raised above the roof surface itself with 'packers', such as offcuts of tanalized roof battening, to ensure that rain runs away to drainage gulleys. Strips of decking timber are then fixed at right angles to the joists, normally spaced 40cm/15in apart, by counter-sinking screws or rustproof nails, with a gap between timbers of around 10mm/ in. In some situations a deck need not be fixed to a complex sub-structure but, if placed on a level surface, will remain stable due to its own weight. Thanks to its simplicity of construction, decking can often be cut into to make way for additional beds as the garden develops.

1 An interlinked series of stained wooden decks takes four gradual steps up to the rear of this small enclosed garden and disappears beneath the tangled stems of *Actinidia chinensis*. The detail evident in the alternating direction of timbers from deck to deck contrasts with a bold and exotic planting of acers, hostas, ferns, aucuba and fatsia that sits well against this dominant element.

2 The use of metal grilles to make a deck with welded blocks of sheet–steel furniture provides for a contemporary and innovative industrial look in this unusual seating area.

3 A deck is used here almost to define the presence of the garden. There is an illusion of simple intervention with nature as the deck stretches out as if to assert territory over its watery surrounds. But in reality this deck is far from simple: it holds a swimming pool and seating areas.

4 A raised boardwalk strides out along the side of a sloping site, leading towards the sea. It gives access to a secluded seat surrounded by plants.

'Descendant of the porches of ancient Japanese dwellings, decks bring lighter tones to dark, shaded gardens'

Overhead features

With the depletion of the ozone layer, shade is a growing concern in temperate areas, especially for gardeners with young children. In hot countries plants like vines and scented climbers have long adorned pergolas, arches and arbours to provide respite from the sun's rays. This has enabled people to spend time outdoors with unimpeded views, without being directly exposed to the sun overhead.

A pergola is a succession of freestanding arches usually made from sturdy upright supporting posts of brick or timber with lighter rafters of timber or metal to support plants trained overhead. With a clear head space of around 2.2m/7ft (remember that flowers hanging down reduce head clearance), pergolas often cover walkways and can be connected to a building or a freestanding structure at one end. Constructed from large brick pillars and thick oak beams, a pergola can be a sturdy architectural feature in, say, a formal garden. Made from a series of thin metal hoops or pairs of hazel poles joined at their apex to make arches, a pergola will merge with other features in a romantic or carefree design. A bamboo structure dripping with the large, bright trumpet flowers of campsis and sweetly scented star jasmine will increase the lavish sense of enclosure of an exotic oasis. Pergolas entice us along pathways with the promise of an ultimate view or destination. This can continue the journey to other parts of the garden or finish with a feature like a fountain, sculpture or a piece of topiary.

An arbour is a framework building that, once overgrown with plants, offers natural shade and shelter, becoming part building, part climbing frame for plants. It is the ideal place for a moment's quiet thought, enshrouded with delicate blooms, soft foliage and intoxicating scent in a romantic garden. Fun for adults and children alike, an arbour feels rather like a tree house brought to earth, bringing an added dimension to any fantasy or carefree garden – somewhere safe and secluded to escape to, surrounded by plants, where you can spend hours observing accompanying bird and insect life. All these structures allow us to enjoy scent and colour from climbing plants such as wisteria, jasmine, roses and honeysuckle.

1

1 Although the supporting metal framework of this large arch has entirely disappeared beneath the vigorous growth of a rambling rose, the structure is sturdy enough to hold the considerable weight of its decorative burden. Bear this in mind when you match a climber to any support you wish it to grow over. Though it may appear rather solid and unappealing when newly planted, it will ultimately end up invisible, as in this image.

2 In a shaded, leafy, open-sided arbour, plants combine with an ornate metal framework to make a well-camouflaged, verdant

3

retreat. Surrounded by foliage, this seating area has an intimate, magical feel but is spacious enough for two.

3 Pergolas can range from a narrow procession of posts and cross-beams over a small pathway to this vast, spreading structure that creates shade for an expansive terrace via a tangled ceiling of wisteria stems. Using a deciduous climber means that the pergola provides shade when it is most needed in summer and lets in light in the darker months of autumn and winter when stems are bare.

'An arbour, once overgrown with plants, offers natural shade and shelter; it feels rather like a tree house brought to earth'

Garden buildings

Buildings such as summer houses, gazebos, greenhouses and even the humble shed can become points of focus and reference that entice us into gardens. Familiar oases of shelter and sanctuary in verdant surroundings, they add a sense of proportion and bring to our gardens a human scale. Without them, gardens can be merely places for show rather than occupation. As well as being somewhere from which to observe the garden and in which to shelter and entertain, or to store tools and machinery, garden buildings can play an important part in the garden's overall look. Whenever possible, they should be treated as design elements like any other feature, so that they make a positive aesthetic contribution to a garden.

Summer houses and gazebos are often highly stylized, particularly in gardens with a strong design theme. At one extreme, these buildings may appear as leading features, for example an oriental-inspired tea house in an exotic or Zen style of garden. In formal and minimal garden styles, the presence of a bold, sleek glass and steel summer house may play a more prominent role in the overall design than the plants themselves, whereas in a carefree garden a timber summer house is likely to be camouflaged and enshrouded with planting so that it visually recedes.

Sheds may be painted or clad with trellis and climbing plants to take on decorative detail and give the illusion of a higher purpose. To suit more relaxed styles, they should be treated to merge with their surroundings. A turf roof, for example, can camouflage a garden shed, turning it into a pleasing feature with a crown of grasses and wildflowers that distracts from a purely functional role. Wendy houses, studios, offices, saunas, dens and retreats are just a few of the many manifestations of garden buildings. Some of these uses can be strongly signalled by an exterior design or finish; others can be a complete surprise, lurking behind the everyday veneer of a common or garden shed. There are occasions when a garden shed will need to be hidden from view, so ensure that you reserve space in a secluded spot for this essential yet aesthetically awkward element.

■ With its glass roof, slender beams and open sides, this gazebo takes full advantage of its natural setting with as little structural intrusion as possible. Such a building can extend the hours of garden usage into night-time when illuminated, and into the months when wetter weather is common, thanks to the protection of its roof. Ideal as a setting for meals as well as for relaxation, such a structure allows for maximum enjoyment of the garden around it.

4

2 The shelter of an extended roof provides for a handy storage area as well as an intimate seating corner. Where space is at a premium, as in a small plot, such constructive and creative use of available features can go a long way to diversifying the experience of a garden.

3 With a little imagination your garden building can take on the guise of something outlandish, even awe-inspiring. Cladding with trellis and climbers, painting, or re-facing with textured timber sheeting can all make a big difference to a shed. Or you can build for the extraordinary from the start, as has been done here with this magical outdoor play house for children.

4 A building such as this small summer house can personalize a corner in any carefree garden – large or small – as it takes architecture out into wilder areas. This can often make the building a focal point that contributes to the design and feel of the garden as well as widening the range of activities possible in the garden,

'Familiar oases of shelter and sanctuary in verdant surroundings, garden buildings add a sense of proportion and bring to our gardens a human scale'

Steps and gates

Providing an entrance or a link between different parts of a garden, steps and gates often indicate where one section ends and another begins. They may also be used effectively to bridge contrasting styles. For example, where a garden comprises terraces on several levels, steps become an important link, not only providing access but also performing a design role in extending lines to create visual patterns through the garden.

In a formal design, steps may be placed symmetrically at either end of a terrace made perhaps from sawn stone, hardwood decking or textured glass. Whatever materials you choose, clean lines and uniform construction should be the main concern. In an informal design, steps are likely to be placed unobtrusively, following the natural contour of an incline, and made from materials that blend in with the surroundings. Broad steps made from organic materials such as stone slabs, logs or railway sleepers may be used to link sections of a wild garden. They might even be filled with soil and planted with annual flowers and grasses or, in a herb garden, with thyme and Corsican mint, providing an unusual walking surface that blends in with its surroundings. In a dry 'desert' garden, steps may be no more than pieces of timber with soil banked up behind them to make dusty, natural-looking treads. Narrow steps with tiny treads add mystery to a garden as they invite us to tiptoe to unknown destinations; they may be included purely as a visual ploy to make a garden seem larger or more mysterious, while actually leading nowhere. Broad steps can be used as a platform for containers or as additional seating in small gardens, or might be kept clear and unembellished in a minimal design.

Gates allow selective admission into the garden and, when closed, make it a safe place for children to play. Sturdy gates have always been a great place to stop and chat and can form a welcome break in the continuum of a fence, hedge or other boundary marker. An austere wrought iron or galvanized steel gate might form an appropriate entry to a formal garden, while decorative painted timber gates are often used in romantic gardens. In a recycled or carefree garden gates may be threadbare at best, allowing planting to show through so the presence of a barrier is relatively imperceptible.

'Steps and gates may be used effectively to provide an entrance or a link between separate parts of a garden or to bridge contrasting styles within it'

1 This rural gateway, made using wood prunings, has an almost transient appearance, as though assembled to last no more than a few years. It denotes access and boundary with a subtle beauty and no great sense of permanence.

2 Simple, broad steps filled with gravel and retained by timber make a comfortable-looking progression through this garden. With their generous width and depth, they mark a breathing space amid the excitement and intensity of the exotic plants around.

3 The relationship between these two wooden gates with matching geometric detailing creates an enhanced perspective that adds depth to the view through a gap in an old stone wall. The silvery tones of weathered oak add to the character of these features.

4 The dramatic lines of industrial architecture can be effective in a modern minimal garden, as seen in this spiral staircase. Wherever the variety and complexity of planting and other elements are reduced, such structural features take on an intense presence.

5 The quality of materials can be enough to reward the eye. These beautiful steps, crafted from stone, snake upwards through the long grasses.

decoration

Trellis and plant supports

Many plants, notably climbers, need support to get them above ground level. In their natural habitat plants such as climbing roses and jasmine will be found growing up, against and over trees and shrubs as a means of reaching the sunlight. In gardens we create similar situations by planting rambling roses through old fruit trees and up dead stumps or training clematis against sunny walls. As we seek to create our own piece of nature through collecting various plants together, we can go further by deliberately placing structures that double up as decorative features as well as climbing frames for plants.

Within a garden, trellis panels can form a subtle internal division or can be used to raise the height of boundary walls to increase seclusion. They may be placed to create intimate inner zones within, say, a romantic garden, where their structure can gently define a boundary, enclose a seating area or make up an arbour, while at the same time forming a living structure adorned with scented roses, honeysuckle and clematis. As unembellished design features in themselves, trellis panels can add strong lines to draw out the sense of serenity and order in a Zen or formal garden. Trellis protects planting, often acting as a windbreak on a roof terrace, and allows glimpses of what lies beyond as well as letting light through to plants and garden on both sides. Made of smooth, prepared timbers, rustic branches, intricate metalwork or woven reeds, trellis can perform its role in many different guises to suit the particular style of a garden.

Obelisks, wigwams and other such structures have a strong architectural presence and focus attention on the plants they support by appearing as formalized features in a bed or border. Made from painted thin metal strips or latticed timber with decorative finials, they rise up above lower-level planting. These decorative supports can become an element of control and order when placed at regular intervals along large borders or in the corners of small plots to create a sense of formality, or they may be no more than a bunch of hazel rods tied together and placed randomly about a garden, covered with plants, to give a less ordered appearance. Careful positioning will ensure they make a contribution to the garden's structure even in winter.

1 A slender obelisk of welded metal rods, topped with a ball, casts an elegant rusted profile amid sweet peas and fennel stems. Features such as this, that are left out to weather, maintain a presence in the garden all year round. They form an important decoration as planting recedes and the garden becomes bare in winter, while they quickly become blurred and indistinct, disappearing behind a rush of foliage in the growing season.

'As we seek to create our own piece of nature through collecting various plants together, we can go further by deliberately placing structures that double up as decorative features as well as climbing frames for plants'

unique and more appealing. Try alternating panels of different mesh sizes and patterns – say, squares and diamonds. Alternatively,

as has been done here, paint the panels and posts in a colour that suits your design and planting to ensure a smarter appearance.

2 As a stylish means of compartmentalizing a garden, trellis has much to offer, forming a decorative divider that is less dominating than a fence or a wall. Any number of patterns can be created, from loose, organic irregular shapes made with willow whips bound into a hazel framework to the precise geometric patterns of architectural trellis panels that often appear alongside topiary in formal designs.

Here, an ivy–clad arched trellis panel features a mirror that gives the illusion of another garden room beyond it.

3 Trellis need not be prohibitive in cost, though it is important to ensure that the panels you buy are sturdy and solid, rather than flimsy. With a little additional exertion, a few run–of–the–mill panels can be trans-formed into something

Sculpture and ornament

Sculpture and other ornamental features are often very personal additions to a garden, but they all enliven dull corners and create focal points that hold the eye so that attention slowly settles on those plants and elements that surround them. They bring atmosphere to a garden whether they are bold, subtle, stylish, humorous, or even shocking. Some will take time to become integrated within a garden, requiring constant re-siting until you find the right place for them, whereas others will instantly be the 'key' that locks the whole garden together and expresses its essential spirit.

Unless the object is intended to shock, it is important to consider its contribution carefully and to place it with a degree of subtlety. Sculpture and ornament can risk appearing too obvious: placed a little too far to the left or right, say, they may all too easily jar with everything else that succeeds in the garden. However, an appropriate choice, well placed, can bring the perfect finishing touch to a garden, focusing the finer details of design and acting as an effective foil to the planting and other structural details. Good placement does not necessarily mean simply siting a piece of sculpture at the end of a vista or axis; it could be just as effective displayed on a wall or tucked in a corner of the garden.

A weather-worn block of stone can convey a powerful sense of nature in its shape, linking it to other natural forms, while more stylized statuary such as busts and classical figures bring with them a symbolic, historical context and atmosphere. A piece of contemporary sculpture might embolden a formal layout or become the inspiration for a striking conceptual design. If made from natural materials, pieces will develop the patina of age and will change their appearance in different lights and with the seasons – but all sculpture and ornament has a permanent, year-round presence. Found objects such as pieces of machinery, driftwood or other salvaged items can be transformed into pieces of eclectic beauty, strange character and maverick humour when placed out of context in a recycled garden. A piece of sculpture might become the 'ringmaster' to a fantasy garden where shrubs clipped into extraordinary topiary shapes assume a life of their own beyond their existence as plants.

1 Sculpture can dominate any part of a garden, adding character and atmosphere wherever it appears. Here, a colourful, rotund ceramic figure covered in a decorative grid-like pattern of blue and silver mosaic squares strides forth from a flower bed.

2 The enjoyment of a garden may often be sealed through the detail in the smallest plants and features. Thin golden rods capped with snail shells in a low-level colourful planting tell of one gardener's attention to decoration.

3 The placing of sculpture is all-important for maximum impact. A sympathetic combination – of, say, wooden carvings in an exotic planting – can be effective. But so, too,

5

'Sculpture and other ornamental features

can the sensitive juxtaposition depicted here, where a seductive round piece of carved stone balances the linear pattern of the grasses.

4 If it has enough character, sculpture will place itself in the garden. This metal alligator looks entirely at home guarding a large pond.

5 Not all ornament need be bought at great cost. Here, a group of curving bamboo-like stems forms an intimate relationship with the branching trunk of a nearby tree.

all enliven dull corners and create focal points'

Containers

Containers make a garden mobile. As long as you can lift them, they and their contents may be moved around to take the tone and texture of plants to different areas. And as a single container can be filled with any type of soil or compost mix, they allow for a variety of plants with different growing and nutritional requirements to be placed together. Containers are ideal for bulbs that have relatively short flowering periods; they can be brought into the limelight for their flowering time, then removed to a less prominent place or the pots planted up for later interest. Pots filled with tulips, for example, can be placed in beds in spring to fill gaps and add colour and height while the green shoots of summer-flowering perennials around them slowly head skywards. Containers also bring plants closer to the eye and nose, allowing you to appreciate the intricate beauty of plants at close quarters and offering their scent wherever you may wish it. They can also raise the succulent leaves of foliage plants away from hungry slugs and other pests to relative safety.

A container may be a garden in itself. A window box on a ledge high up in a city tower block can become a beautiful and enchanting microcosm of natural pleasures or a pot beside a kitchen door a Provençal herb garden. Tender plants such as citrus trees can be moved outside during warm weather, then brought inside to a room or conservatory when temperatures drop. Architectural plants look all the more striking in containers made from steel or glazed pottery and clipped topiary pieces suit smart wooden Versailles-style planters or lead containers (lead is an expensive material, so consider the cheaper resin substitutes if your budget is tight). Ubiquitous terracotta is light and relatively inexpensive, its tones matching well with most plant foliage and flowers.

A garden may be made entirely from plants in containers – say, on a roof where there is no soil available or in gardens where the soil is very poor. Grouped together, pots give the effect of a dense massed planting, suitable for a carefree or romantic garden, while spaced evenly in rows or with sparse intervals between them they can enhance a formal or minimal layout. For the beginner, the beauty of pots is that they allow for planting combinations to be tested over time before committing to long-term planting in beds.

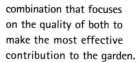

1 In the dry, minimal garden where this picture was taken, the planting extends no further than these few selected cacti in their container. In such a case it is vital to match the plants to their receptacle as perfectly as possible: look for a striking combination that focuses on the quality of both to make the most effective contribution to the garden.

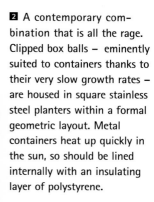

2 A contemporary combination that is all the rage. Clipped box balls – eminently suited to containers thanks to their very slow growth rates – are housed in square stainless steel planters within a formal geometric layout. Metal containers heat up quickly in the sun, so should be lined internally with an insulating layer of polystyrene.

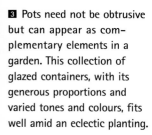

3 Pots need not be obtrusive but can appear as complementary elements in a garden. This collection of glazed containers, with its generous proportions and varied tones and colours, fits well amid an eclectic planting.

4 The restricted space of a window box need not inhibit your planting ambitions. Here, a blue-painted wooden trough has been filled with a variety of drought-resistant succulent plants to make a small garden of great impact.

'A container may be a garden it itself. A window box on a ledge high up in a city tower block can become a beautiful and enchanting microcosm of natural pleasures or a pot beside a kitchen door a Provençal herb garden.'

Seating

A seat could be considered the most essential item as far as gardeners are concerned – a place from which to enjoy the spectacle of our labours! We are naturally drawn to seats and benches as points of repose on our journey through a garden and a pleasant seat in the right place will open a garden up to gentle, passive enjoyment by visitors.

When placed in pairs alongside or opposite one another, seats can introduce a sense of symmetrical formality to any style of garden. Wherever they are placed, they focus attention in the direction they face. A large wall or hedge that might be somewhat disproportionate on the boundary of a small plot can be 'brought into' the garden layout by a seat placed in front of it, facing inwards. A seat can also add to the experience of a garden when positioned to draw the eye out to the wider landscape that is 'borrowed' for those who stop to rest and contemplate the view.

As design features in themselves, seats can dominate a garden with strong, seductive lines or mimic natural structures when made from rustic timbers or woven branches. They can become living elements, in the form of turf or herb seats or when fashioned from willow wands that will take root in the soil and sprout shoots and leaves. Seating may be built into the structure of a garden, perhaps included in a series of raised beds where it will become surrounded by plants, or it may stand alone as an almost sculptural feature on a raised platform.

In a carefree or romantic garden, a felled tree left to rot in a quiet corner will make a seat that will last for many years before it becomes dust and returns to the ground. Old car seats, a pile of bricks or even railway sleepers can – with the accompaniment of a few cushions – become surprising places of rest in a recycled garden. Think about the degree of comfort you desire and the extent to which your seating will become a design feature, then go in search of furniture to match your requirements. Consider the best views from your seating and assess how the furniture itself will appear from other areas; the majority of garden furniture is mobile so that if you don't get it right first time, you can simply try again in a new location.

1

4

1 Stark minimalism rules the layout of this striking seating area. The use of natural slate for seats and a thick sheet of glass for a table-top is complemented by the cylindrical stainless steel containers holding their architectural black bamboos. This area has obviously been designed primarily for visual impact, with comfort perhaps a not-so-close second.

2 A secluded corner of a timber balcony is the perfect site for this cosy grouping of table and chairs. With a welcoming and informal atmosphere, the combination of plants, bright textiles and simple furniture make for an alluring and decorative assembly.

3 In assuming the colour of the paving material on which it stands, this sleek stone bench recedes from the eye into a gentle balance with the topiary balls that flank it. Creating built-in furniture in this way, so that it becomes to a degree absorbed by surrounding features, allows it to become an unexpected surprise when discovered. This can greatly help to develop a sense of diversification in a small garden.

4 A simple seat in the right place is all that is needed. Here, in a sunny spot with water to gaze at and something to sit back into, the placement seems to say it all.

'We are naturally drawn to seats and benches as places of rest on our journey through a garden and a seat in the right place will open a garden up to passive enjoyment'.

Garden lighting

Thanks to candles, lanterns and modern lighting equipment, the pleasures of a garden need not be consigned purely to daylight hours. Lighting extends the domestic interior outdoors after dark, enabling us to negotiate our gardens when the weather permits. At the same time it shows us an altered image of the garden, since colours and textures change and modify under artificial light. Some form of lighting can enhance the garden's focal points by picking them out at night – by this means the contents of the garden will appear pared down as the eye is guided by where the light falls.

Night lighting can be naturalistic, with candles in windproof glass housings or oil lanterns on stakes casting moving shadows about a garden as flames flicker and create subtle illumination. A discreet low-voltage electrical system with fittings hidden in beds can cast a gentle wash of light over plants or up into trees with magical effect, and focus can be drawn to a shrub or architectural specimen when it is picked out by a spotlight or back-lit. The structure of trees themselves can become a night-time feature with strings of small lights run out along their limbs; the effect can be startlingly beautiful where several subjects are lit in this way, especially when the garden is dormant and many trees are bare in winter months. A more subtle, painterly approach may be achieved through the use of sympathetic lighting to show off the style of planting rather than being a feature in itself.

On the other hand, lighting can become as much a feature of the design at night as the plants and structures themselves. The fittings may be very visible – for instance, large frosted-glass balls fixed to a wall, or light panels incorporated in the risers of steps to make a design statement while providing safe visible access. Light can enhance a design by night when elements such as water features, steps, seating and trellis are illuminated or back-lit to show strong silhouettes or to cast complex shadows on walls and flooring.

Safety is paramount where electric lighting is concerned: install circuit breakers at all power points. Ideally you should use low-voltage equipment, connected through transformers to the mains supply. A sizeable system will require the services of an electrician and a professional lighting designer.

1 With bold and sculptural features – such as these two box balls in stoneware pots – simple lighting has a great effect. The downlighter above accentuates the dimpled uniformity of the clipped balls in contrast with the smooth wall behind them, bringing an altered focus from that experienced in the daytime.

2 Lighting can add a unique perspective to our visual appreciation of a garden. With attention focused only on those features that are illuminated, the designer or owner of a garden can show it off in the way they feel is most stimulating and effective. Here the pool and its surround are picked out by uplighters at night.

3 As darkness falls, coloured bulbs and lenses bring magical fairy-light decoration into a garden designed by Topher Delaney for the San Diego Children's Hospital and help to identify features and indicate different areas. Here, a wall comes to life with a flickering procession of bright lights that runs across its face.

'Lighting can enhance the garden's focal points by picking them out at night – the contents of the garden will appear pared down as the eye is guided by where the light falls'

4 Concealed fittings, like these lights on spikes stuck into the soil amid planting, can create exciting shadows and illumination. In this sunken bed of grasses three such lights throw a pattern of light interspersed with enlarged shadows across a wall, giving what appears in daytime as a delicate planting a bolder, more dramatic profile.

the design process

Having assessed the plot in which you are going to create a garden, as discussed in the first chapter, you will have made notes about your initial feelings as to what could work. From this basic inspection, you have then explored the possibilities of a variety of garden styles and contemplated an array of practical and decorative elements with which to furnish it.

It is quite probable that, during the process of seeking inspiration, visualizing your dream and assembling the elements of your garden design, you will have drawn up a wish list that far exceeds what your garden, and perhaps your budget, can accommodate. So with this mass of information now starting to become consolidated within a design framework – whether in a scrapbook, on a large sheet of paper or simply in your mind's eye – it is important to begin relating back to the plot in which everything is to be assembled. The design process thus becomes a period of selection in which you retain what is essential to the ultimate success of your garden and start to decide where things will go and how they will look. Along the way, other less appropriate ingredients and ideas will get discarded.

For reference, keep your sources of inspiration – books, photographs, sketches and notes – to hand throughout. From this point on, your aim is to develop, and commit to paper, a working design around the ideas and elements you have chosen, allocating each of them enough space for their impact to be appreciated.

Trying out your ideas

The single most important part of the design process is being able to visualize your key ideas and images as a cohesive combination that will produce your ideal garden. I find it useful at this stage to experiment with a series of impression sketches that show how my different ideas might work within the confines of the garden before me. For the virgin gardener, the challenge is to commit all your ideas to paper, drawing what you have imagined with a realistic degree of scale and perspective.

The key to saving long hours struggling with correct perspective lies before you in your very own plot – all you need to do is photograph it, using, if possible, a wide-angled lens. Position yourself so that you get the best view of your garden through the camera. If you can't frame the plot in one shot, take several pictures to make a composite image. Place tracing paper over the developed print/s and draw on the major existing features such as walls, fences, sheds, pergolas and planting. Enlarge this tracing on a photocopier until it is roughly A4-sized, then use this outline to guide you as you test out your different design combinations.

Placing another sheet of tracing paper over the garden outline, use a pencil to draw in the new scheme. Start with important areas and features such as lawn, beds, hard surfaces and architectural structures. Keep reworking the drawing as you add more detail until everything fits and you have a framework for your design. Eventually you will refine your ideas into a finished drawing that shows clearly what words simply could not describe.

First photograph your plot. Find an angle for the image that includes as many as possible of the key features, such as walls, trellis and trees. Also ensure that the image incorporates the boundaries of the plot, even if these are disguised by plantings. In the garden shown here, a pier emerging through shrubs on the right hand side of the garden indicates the line of the boundary and is therefore crucial to the image.

Place tracing paper over the photograph and trace an outline of the garden's important features. Where lines disappear in areas of planting or behind unwanted structures, simply extend them to where the perspective in the photograph guides you. Enlarge the tracing on to an A4 sheet of paper, using a photocopier, so that you can make as many different impression sketches as you have ideas.

Using a pencil, draw in the new elements of the garden on tracing paper over the enlarged outlines of the plot. At this stage you can afford to be quite messy – keep your sketches alive, rubbing out and reworking them as you add details and features from your wish list.

With several to choose from, you may now be able to select one or two rough sketches to take on to a final stage. Placing them under a fresh piece of tracing paper, copy the lines of the new elements of your design carefully in ink, then add to these the boundaries and original features you wish to retain, where they are still visible.

Drawing your layout

Now that you can see how your design works as an artistic impression on paper, the time has come to tie it in with a degree of accuracy to the actual layout of the site. With a combination of your impression sketch and accurate measurements taken from the garden itself (see opposite), you can draw up a design layout depicting the garden's existing features such as boundaries, contours and levels and including the location and surface area of new beds, hard surfaces, paths and structures. If done to scale, this drawing will be a great help in specifying the number of plants you will need (see pages 126–7), and the quantity of such materials as topsoil, turf and brick paviors. With such detailed information, it will be easier to explain elements of the design to any contractors you might employ. To make your layout understandable to others, it is helpful to use a set of symbols, with an explanatory key, to represent the important features. Below are the symbols I generally use.

Key to symbols

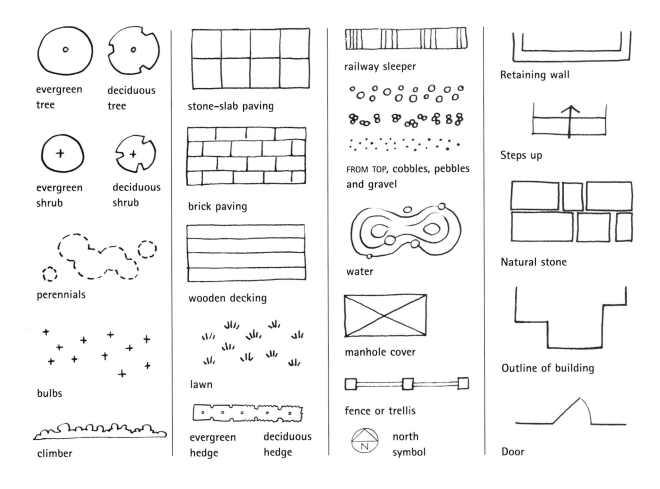

evergreen tree	deciduous tree	
evergreen shrub	deciduous shrub	
perennials		
bulbs		
climber		

stone-slab paving

brick paving

wooden decking

lawn

evergreen hedge | deciduous hedge

railway sleeper

FROM TOP, cobbles, pebbles and gravel

water

manhole cover

fence or trellis

north symbol

Retaining wall

Steps up

Natural stone

Outline of building

Door

Taking dimensions

Take several measurements across the site in order to use a scaled-down version of them to depict accurate dimensions within the design layout (see page 120). To measure up, mark out the garden at 1m intervals around the boundary and, if you wish, draw a chequerboard of 1m squares across the whole plot with pegs. This makes it easier to relate the actual site to a sheet of paper marked out in 1cm squares. If your scale is 1:100, 1m on site will become 1cm on paper; if it is 1:200, 2m will become 1cm – and so on. In an irregular garden, try to separate areas into geometric shapes and then estimate any other curved or random shapes.

Draw the garden's boundaries on to the design layout and mark on existing features such as trees and beds that you intend to incorporate in the new garden. Then draw in your new design, starting with the largest features, such as walls, flower beds, lawns, paved areas and water features. Using a scale ruler will help you to represent all features and elements in correct proportion to the dimensions of the garden (see the two dimensional design layouts overleaf).

At this stage in drawing up your design layout, be prepared for a little further fall-out: you may realize that certain items are too close together or that they interfere with existing features. Notice how, when one element is taken out, it changes the relationship between those that remain. For example, you may decide that the central pathway you liked in a formal design actually creates an uncomfortable symmetry when applied to your own garden. So, in order to avoid an overriding sense of formality and prevent the garden being broken into two halves, you may decide to move the path to one side. Have the confidence to experiment at this stage and to try out several different combinations and interpretations.

Mark the direction of north on the design layout so you can reassess some of the information gleaned while identifying the conditions of the site (see pages 12–13), such as the best spots for sun-loving and shade-tolerant plants, as well as a place in sun or dappled shade for seating. Indicate where tall buildings or overhanging trees may create conditions of dry shade or a problem with surface roots.

Using contractors

If the design involves hidden services such as water or electricity, has a complex arrangement of hard surfaces and water features or you have a very irregularly shaped plot, you may need to commission a landscape architect to draw technical layout plans so that several contractors can quote to carry out specific works. This needs to be an accurate drawing containing detailed specifications and may include cross-sections through steps, walls and hard surfaces.

Should you need to employ a contractor, it is a good idea to draw up a written specification of what you want doing, together with copies of any relevant drawings, and ask each contractor for a quotation in writing. This should state exactly what they will do for the price they are quoting, along with an estimated time scale for the completion of tasks. The quotation should specify particular types of materials, be it reclaimed red bricks, 10mm beach pebbles or tanalized timber, to ensure that you end up with exactly what you expect. You will generally be asked to pay an amount on deposit, with possibly an interim payment and a final sum on completion.

The design layout

Below are examples of design layouts drawn up for two quite different gardens. For the long, narrow plot (right), a scale of 1:100 fits the drawing on to the page. The smaller L-shaped garden (below) is drawn to a scale of 1:50 – that allows finer details to be shown. The larger the garden, the smaller the scale needed to show it on one piece of paper. To read fine details you will need a larger scale, and perhaps to focus on individual areas of the garden in a series of separate drawings.

• Drawing your design layout on tracing paper over a grid can help you to plot the dimensions, especially where there are many curved lines.

• Do several pencil roughs as you try to get things to fit. When you have arrived at a successful layout, trace over it in ink.

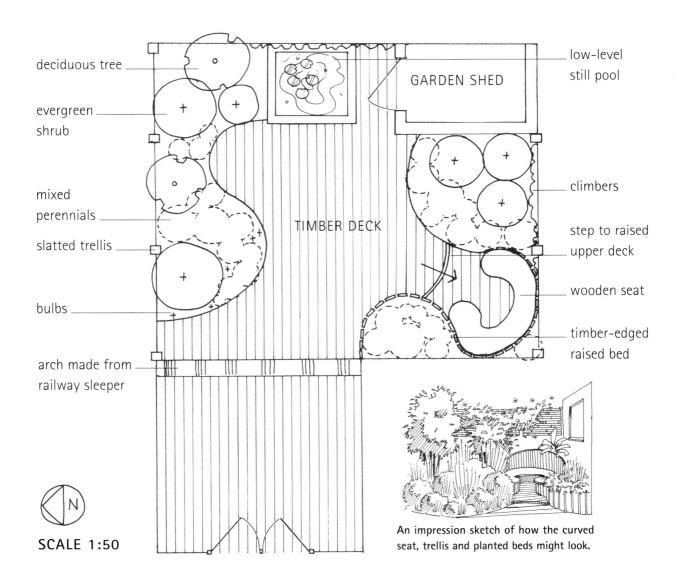

deciduous tree

evergreen shrub

mixed perennials

slatted trellis

bulbs

arch made from railway sleeper

GARDEN SHED

TIMBER DECK

low-level still pool

climbers

step to raised upper deck

wooden seat

timber-edged raised bed

SCALE 1:50

An impression sketch of how the curved seat, trellis and planted beds might look.

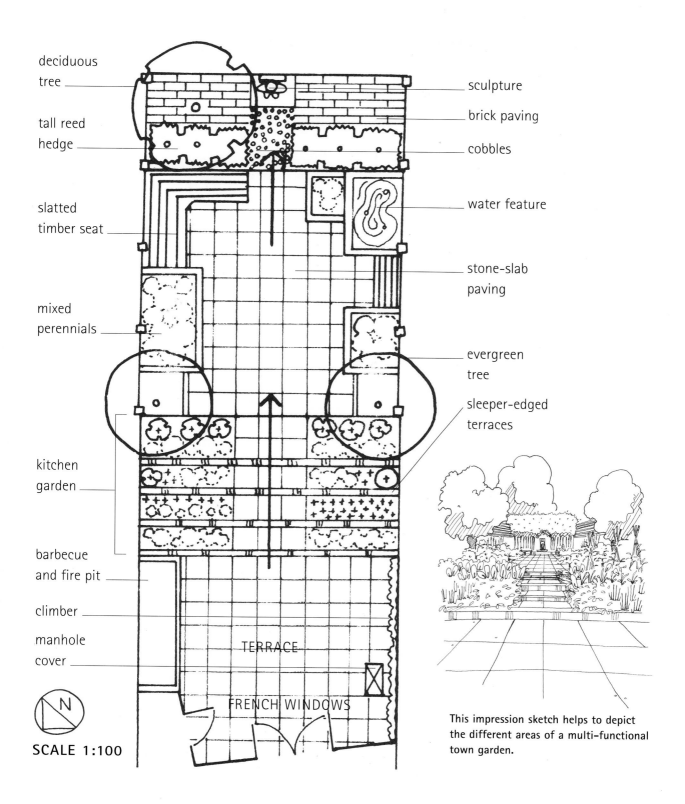

deciduous tree

tall reed hedge

slatted timber seat

mixed perennials

kitchen garden

barbecue and fire pit

climber

manhole cover

sculpture

brick paving

cobbles

water feature

stone-slab paving

evergreen tree

sleeper-edged terraces

TERRACE

FRENCH WINDOWS

SCALE 1:100

This impression sketch helps to depict the different areas of a multi-functional town garden.

Mocking up your design layout

It is important to try and imagine how the division and reorganization of your outdoor space – visualized in both impression sketches and a design layout – will work in the reality of the garden. Now that your ideas have become fairly fixed, it is worth going outdoors for a last check before committing yourself irrevocably to anything. By roughly marking out the intended framework, you will be able to 'stroll around' your drawings and assess your design's practicality and suitability on the ground.

Using a line of sand, a length of garden hose, a pattern of twigs or spray-on line, mark out on the ground the approximate outline of boundaries, beds, lawns, paved surfaces and other such ground-based features. Walk through this imaginary landscape and make alterations where you find the dimensions of any lawns or beds uncomfortable in some way, whether too small, too large or the wrong shape. Try to imagine the outline of other features in solid terms, rising into the proportions of whatever feature – seat, shed, border or pergola – they detail. Keep working with these lines until you feel confident that their arrangement convincingly translates your design ideas into the garden.

Where possible, look down on to the marked-out garden from a vantage point, such as an upper floor window, to check that the layout works visually as well as functionally. To give your 'site sketch' a more three-dimensional feel, place cardboard boxes, tea chests, furniture and other such items where key features such as seats, topiary and sculpture might go. Use stakes with rope or string tied between them to delineate the position of fences, walls or trellis. Then take another stroll round the garden to see that it feels right.

Do not expect everything to seem perfect from the outset. I often find there is a single element I am sure about, such as the siting of the large wooden bench in my own garden, while everything else spins around in a whirr of uncertainty for quite some time. The more I work at it, adding and moving elements around, the more they start to settle and find their place. Most important of all is to develop a sense of open space in the layout to allow for such features as table and chairs, raised beds and structures to have their full effect. Whatever you decide to include, you will find that seating areas and beds for planting will ultimately take up more room than you might have imagined.

If time permits, leave your trial assemblage in the garden for a day or so and return to it afresh to see whether any part of the layout feels blank, constricted or over-crammed. The space itself should indicate to you what you can and cannot eventually fit in, so keep stepping back to see how the whole picture is working. If something doesn't feel right, this is unlikely to change, so remove it and see what new opportunities this creates.

When you are satisfied that the space works and everything in your mock-up locks together, you can feel confident that the garden will be all you had hoped for. If any major alterations take place at this stage, you should do a revised design layout and plan of work to keep everything up to date.

The entire creation of a garden need not be resolved on paper. Here the placing of a large seat in my own garden became a stimulus for the design of adjoining areas. Once the seat had found a niche between two trees, it spurred on the creation of broad curving beds; I used hazel rods driven into them to mirror its structural presence.

Basic planting design

I have always found planting the best part of designing and making a garden. There is a great thrill in putting into your soil living elements that will grow and develop to turn an outline into a vital, ever-changing environment. This process is greatly enhanced by good preparation of the soil and the confidence that what you are doing is correct and plant-friendly. To make sure of this, there are a few important considerations worth bearing in mind that govern the positioning and grouping of plants in even the most random, carefree and chaotic of designs.

Plants all have different characteristics (see the various categories within the Plant manifesto) and grow at varying speeds to different forms and with a preference for certain conditions. These must be considered when arranging trees, shrubs, climbers, perennials, bulbs and annuals in your beds and borders, as well as in water features and containers. To help, use your design layout, which already shows the dimensions of planting areas. By drawing on to this you can space out and quantify the plants you wish to include. It will make things easier if you do enlarged drawings of the various planting areas to an increased scale, so that even small perennials can be shown in their position.

It is best to commence your planting plan with the largest plants such as trees and large shrubs; these will establish a visual structure within which smaller and more detailed items such as climbers, small shrubs and perennials will sit. In certain styles the structure can be further strengthened by selecting architectural plants (see pages 176–7) or by introducing shrubs clipped to shape. When making such bold strokes, assess the effect these plants may have on structural elements such as pathways, seating areas and entrances – as well as your neighbours. For instance, a fast-growing evergreen tree such as a eucalyptus, which you might plant in the form of a 2m/6ft 6in sapling, can create a large, beautiful specimen in no time, but it will also cast shade, reduce available moisture for nearby plants and could block the view from windows. As you arrange these larger key items into screens, hedges, natural groupings or individual feature plantings, consider the way in which they will change through the seasons. In many styles, a balanced evergreen structure with year-round interest is of great value, especially in the lean months of winter.

As the main structure develops on your plan, you will be able to assess the space that surrounds it more accurately and plan the next level of 'infill' planting. Smaller shrubs and large perennials will help to fill out and further enhance the richness of your scheme, adding detail, contrast, texture and colour. Look for opportunities to introduce exciting combinations that will enliven your design. For

A rich dense planting in this country garden relies on a balance between roses and other shrubs, evergreen topiary, climbers and a profusion of herbaceous perennials for a cohesive planting full of exuberant contrasts that manages to achieve a sense of structural permanence.

example, *Acer dissectum* can benefit from a bold, evergreen backdrop of yew or Portuguese laurel as a foil to its delicate, feathery foliage. As you link plants together into subtle or striking groupings, be aware of the ultimate size they will reach as well as their preference for sun or shade. If you do not allow enough space between them, certain plants will be over-run and sun-lovers will quickly lose the light as a faster-growing neighbour causes them to grow pale in darkness.

To complete the planting plan, you will need an underplanting of smaller perennials and bulbs to offer the final wave of interest at ground level. This knits the picture together, offering yet more seasonal interest and, in the case of ground cover, a suitable backdrop to focus attention on larger key plants.

Although there is always a desire for a garden to be full and complete in its first year, resist the temptation to over-plant and place subjects too close to one another, unless you have your heart set on a carefree profusion or an impenetrable exotic thicket. The long-term effects of a desire for short-term impact will be hard to correct in formal, minimal and more refined styles as beds and borders become the scene of a frenzied struggle for space.

When it comes to the planting itself, choose a dry day, if possible, some time between autumn and spring – the ideal planting season should be indicated on plant tags or by your plant retailer. When the plants are delivered, place them on the beds to check that the plan will work. Make any necessary alterations before digging them in, starting with the largest items such as trees and progressing through shrubs to perennials (see A time for action, pages 128–61).

A plan of action

Before throwing yourself into the activity of creating a dream garden, hold your enthusiasm for one final task. In order to avoid reaching a point when you suddenly realize that you have laid the lawn before putting down an adjacent patio or planting up a bed - both of which will wreck your fresh green carpet – draw up a plan of work. Think through all proposed tasks and list them in a logical order so that this kind of situation does not arise. The list will also help you assess when to book in deliveries of materials and plants.

An organized plan of work becomes a checklist of jobs culminating in a finished garden and a long drink. With reference to your plan, estimate how long the whole job, or separate parts of it, will take and set aside time accordingly. A typical order of tasks might be as shown below.

With the aid of your design layout (see page 120), you should be able to estimate the quantities of plants and materials you need, by surface area. The plan of work will also enable you to assess the total cost of the project and, as you work this out, this gives you the opportunity to decide how to spread the available funds over the various tasks.

Order of work

▸ Assess provision of waste disposal facilities: find out where local dump is or book a skip.

▸ Remove any trees and shrubs to come out.

▸ Break up paths and demolish hard surfaces, structures and features that will not remain.

▸ Cut back and reshape as necessary those trees, shrubs and perennials that you intend to keep.

▸ Protect any hard surfaces and steps with hardboard sheeting or boards. Tie up loose shrubs, fix boards round any vulnerable tree trunks and mark the position of perennial plantings to prevent accidental damage during construction.

▸ Reading the dimensions from your design layout, mark out the shape of the new design on the ground, using spray-on line (or any of the techniques referred to on page 122).

▸ Clear the surface area of all new planting zones. Where this intrudes on a lawn, cut turf and, if space permits, stack to rot down for use as a soil conditioner.

▸ Dig out foundations for any large features or hard

surfaces - paths, terraces, pools and ponds - and dig through all planting areas (hire a rotovator if needed). This may result in a lot of spoil that could be used in other areas of the garden, or disposed of.

▸ Dig well-rotted compost into all planting areas: book delivery of compost if needed.

▸ Erect trellis, fencing, shed and any other timber structures.

▸ Book delivery of paving materials, sand and cement. Leaving ducts for power and water supplies to outside features, lay hard surfaces such as stone or brick paths and terraces. Construct walls, buildings and pools.

▸ Book delivery of plants and containers. Plant up beds, borders and containers.

▸ Install irrigation system and garden lighting fittings if desired.

▸ Book the delivery of turf and scaffold boards unless sowing from seed. Lay or sow lawn.

▸ Lie down. ↵

This could see you altering or adjusting your spending, perhaps opting for cheaper slabs or bricks in order to spend more money on planting. On your checklist you can apportion the time you have, and the money in your budget, to different tasks so that, if it is not possible to finish everything in one go, the work can readily be broken down and carried out in a logical order.

When the work being carried out to create a new garden involves several different suppliers of materials and plants as well as one or more contractors, a plan of work is invaluable to ensure that everything runs smoothly.

a time for action

At last the mental effort of the design process is over and it is time to start work in the garden. The practical business of gardening is, without doubt, the most enjoyable part – and all the more so if you approach it fully prepared and well organized. The following chapter describes and illustrates the basic procedures involved in the preparation and upkeep of a garden, all of which can be achieved without the need for skilled workmanship or special training. It deals with laying a lawn and with different planting techniques as well as care and maintenance tasks such as pruning, training and pest control.

Depending on the task you are carrying out, there are good and bad times to embark on work in the garden. Although it does not always pay to wait for warm, dry weather - as many tasks are best completed in the autumn, winter and spring - you should try to avoid working the soil when it is wet and waterlogged or you risk compacting the soil as you dig the beds over.

Preparing a bed

The role of beds and borders is twofold: they contribute colours, tones and textures in the plants that they contain and add their outline, size and proportion to the garden's structural layout. Planting beds can connect features and areas as well as helping to blur boundaries and animate the shape of a garden that might otherwise have a hard geometric outline.

Beds cut from an existing lawn are relatively easy to create. They must be large enough to contain your chosen plants while providing them with the right soil and conditions, whether dry or moist, sunny or shaded. Beds are a crucial element within a garden and should not be marginalized, so be generous with their size. Don't worry about the cost of buying plants to fill them – this can be done in stages, using annuals to keep weeds at bay and simple structures to maintain interest as the planting evolves.

If you are enlarging an existing bed or creating a new one where there was hard landscaping, remove the surface material and break up or dig out any hard sub-base. The soil beneath will be heavily compacted, so dig it through thoroughly before adding manure and possibly extra topsoil.

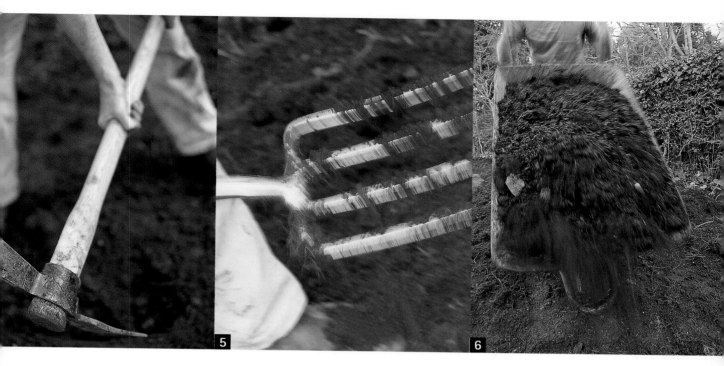

Mark the outline of the bed with rope, a hosepipe or, in this case, sand. You may need to make several attempts. Keep retreating to a vantage point until you are happy that the proportions look right. Here I have marked out a curvaceous bed whose outline was inspired by the shadow cast by an adjacent boundary hedge.

Using a sharp-edged turfing iron or a spade, work your way along the line of the bed, making cuts approximately 8cm/ 3in deep to separate the turf you will remove from that which remains as lawn.

With the spade held horizontally, cut away strips of turf from the area that is to become a bed, rolling them as you go. Stooping as low as is comfortable will make this easier. Try to take off no more than the top 4cm/1½ in of topsoil with the grass. The turf you remove can be unrolled and laid upside down in stacks to rot down over the year into a fine loamy compost.

After years as a lawn, the newly exposed soil will be heavily compacted. Use a mattock (a flat-headed pick, which can be hired) to help break up this surface compaction and to make the next stage easier.

Fork over the bed to a depth of 20cm/ 8in to aerate the soil and ensure that it has enough oxygen available for the roots of new plants. This will also expose the roots of any remaining perennial weeds or grass, as well as revealing rubble that has lain beneath the lawn for years. (Try not to do this when the soil is very wet otherwise your footsteps are likely to re-compact the soil you have just opened up.)

A hungry lawn will have stripped the soil of most of its nutrients, so give the new bed a boost with well-rotted manure or garden compost. Add about six spadefuls per square metre, turning it well into the topsoil.

The cut you made to separate the turf at the initial stage now serves to prevent topsoil from fallling forward on to the grass.

Making a lawn

Preparing the site

First remove all surface foliage. This may involve cutting off an old lawn (see Preparing a bed, page 130) or digging out perennial weeds. Whatever the condition of your site, try not to take away too much good topsoil.

Once cleared of foliage, dig over the area to a depth of about 15cm/6in. This is to break up any compaction of the soil's layers due to previous use, which might prevent new turf from sending roots into the ground beneath it; it also aerates the soil. For large areas you may need to hire a rotovator. Then, using a rake, remove any debris and roots thrown up.

The broken-up soil will now be a mass of clumps and lumps. This rough, open surface needs to be pushed down and gently compacted using your feet. Moving sideways, shuffle along a straight line gently treading the soil down as you go. Then rake the surface to a fine tilth, first in one direction, then at right angles to this. Raking may bring up more debris and rubble that need to be removed. The aim is to end up with a loose, friable and level soil surface.

Seeding a lawn

It is important that the soil for a seeded lawn is prepared to a fine, lump-free consistency, so you may need to rake it a few more times after carrying out the above preparation. Between late spring and mid-autumn, when frosts are not a threat, scatter seed evenly over the soil's surface. This is best done on a calm, dry day by walking in straight lines and broadcasting the seed out to one side. Holding the bag of seed in front of your waist, aim to release the seed in a continual stream as you straighten your arm. As a general rule, use a kilo of seed for about 28 square metres (it's worth keeping some seed back in case there are patches where it does not take first time). Leave the seed on the surface or gently rake it in to ensure contact with

2

3

the topsoil. If necessary place bird scarers around your newly sown area (unwanted CDs suspended on strings work a treat).

Germination takes from a few days to two weeks. During this time you may have to water the seed as the ground should not be allowed to dry out from the time of sowing to the maturing of the completed lawn. It is advisable to stay off a seeded lawn for at least three months. Don't worry about weeds that will almost certainly pop up during this time as mowing will deal with most of them. Give the lawn its first cut after three months.

Turfing a lawn

A turf lawn can be laid at any time of year provided that the ground is not frost-bound and, in hot weather, there is a ready supply of water. To make turf, grass is grown in seed beds for 12–15 months then cut into rolls. All that is needed is for these ready-made sections to take root and secure themselves to your prepared topsoil. Turf is more expensive than seed but has the virtue of being a lawn that can be walked on after only three weeks.

1 Measure the area to be covered and add on 10 per cent to allow for turf wasted through cuts for odd angles or curves. Try to purchase a high-grade utility turf that stays together when unrolled and held by one end. To help the lawn get off to a good start, scatter a general purpose pre-lawn fertilizer on to the soil's surface before the turf goes down.

2 Lay turf as soon as it's delivered. Pile the turves at intervals alongside the prepared area and place boards (these can be hired) next to the rows where you will be laying turf to prevent your having to walk on the prepared ground. Use the board's straight edge to guide the turf as you unroll it.

3 Place your board on top of the line of turf you have just laid and stand on it to lay the next; this gently presses the roots of the grass into the topsoil beneath to encourage rooting; as you proceed along the site, flip the board over.

4 Make sure the edges are firmly butted up against each other to allow for shrinkage in dry weather. Stagger the turf joints, as in brickwork, so that the different sections integrate together more quickly.

TIP Water regularly, if needed, to ensure the turf does not dry out. Whether seeding or turfing, do not overwater a new lawn as this will encourage shallow rooting, causing the lawn to shrivel when conditions become dry. The ideal lawn length is about 3cm/1¼in but keep a new lawn a little longer to retain moisture levels in the soil.

4

1

2

3

Planting trees and shrubs

Planting a bareroot tree

In general it is best to do your planting in the period between late autumn and early spring when plants are dormant, before their roots start to grow, so that transplanting causes little or no damage to the plants themselves and in order that they can get established and benefit from spring showers before the heat of summer arrives. Bareroot trees and shrubs are cheaper than containerized plants and available only when plants are dormant. Plant them as soon as possible after purchasing; if a delay is inevitable, keep their roots under soil in a temporary planting hole. They may be planted in any conditions as long as the soil is not frost-bound.

Dig a hole deep and wide enough to accommodate the tree's roots when spread out. Mix in well-rotted manure or compost with the soil around the hole and stand the tree in the hole so that the soil mark on its stem will be at ground level once planted. Mound the soil slightly at the centre of the hole so that air is not trapped below the roots when you back-fill with soil.

Drive in a tree stake close to the stem to support the bottom third of the tree, and its roots, in windy weather. Tie to the tree with a tree tie that will prevent the wooden stake from chafing the stem. If the tree has a large root system, curl a length of perforated plastic tubing around the roots with an open end above ground level, for more effective watering.

Back-fill the hole and firm the soil round the roots to prevent air pockets that will fill with water and deprive the roots of oxygen. Water in well.

Where a watering pipe is not needed, make a raised rim of soil that allows water to pool around the tree's base.

4

Planting a container-grown shrub

Planting a climber

Dig a hole larger all round than the size of the container and mix well-rotted manure or compost with soil in the hole. Soak the plant in water for 30 minutes, then remove it from the container and gently tease the visible outer roots away from the root mass to encourage them to spread out.

Place the plant in the hole so that its soil surface corresponds with ground level. As with bareroot trees and shrubs, if it is a large specimen a perforated plastic watering tube may need to be curled around the side of the root mass so that watering reaches the whole root system once planted.

If you are planting a container-grown tree, anchor a firm stake in the soil as close to the tree as possible and fasten it with a tree tie, as shown opposite, to support the bottom third of the tree's stem. Then back-fill as for a bareroot tree, creating a dish effect with the soil rim, and water in.

Always soak a climbing plant such as a rose, jasmine or passion flower in water for a few minutes before planting. Dig a hole large enough to accommodate the root mass of the plant along with a generous quantity of well-rotted manure or compost.

Where possible, place the plant at least 45cm/18in away from a wall, fence or other solid form of support to prevent it drying out by being caught in the 'rain shadow' cast by this structure. Lean the plant against the intended support via a wooden cane.

Place a layer of mulch 6–10cm/2½–4in deep (see pages 138–9) around the base of the climber to keep weeds at bay and retain moisture at the roots. As the plant begins to grow, tie in and train its stems as necessary (see Training climbers, pages 144–5).

1

2

Planting containers

Planting up a pot

Any container provides a miniature controlled environment that will accommodate specific growing requirements – such as soil type, drainage and feed levels – for a wide variety of plants. Ensure your container has drainage holes, select a compost that suits the needs of the plants you are potting up, then follow these steps.

Make sure the container you are planting up is at least 5cm/2in wider and deeper than that which the plant is to come out of. Place a 5cm/2in layer of drainage material such as lightweight granules, broken pottery or pebbles in the bottom of the pot to prevent it becoming waterlogged.

Having soaked plants in water for several minutes, remove them from their pots and tease out the roots. You may add slow-release feed granules and water-retentive granules, which expand to hold moisture, to the potting compost. Place enough of this compost mix in the bottom of the new container for the surface of the plant's soil to lie a few centimetres below the rim.

Place the plant in the container and back-fill around the sides with compost. If you are planting a tree or a topiarized shrub with a clear stem you may plant low trailing plants around the base or spread a pebble mulch over the surface of the compost.

> **T I P** As plants grow, they can become pot-bound. To check for this, slip the plant away from the pot. If you see mainly roots, then it is time to pot the plant on by carrying out the above procedures in a larger pot.

3

1

Planting a window box

Select a box that will sit within the confines of your window sill and ensure the masonry is sound enough to support the filled container's weight.

First place a 3cm/1¼in layer of drainage material (see 1, opposite) in the bottom of the window box, then half-fill the box with a multi-purpose compost. As the ratio of soil to plants in window boxes can be very low and they are often placed on exposed sills high above the ground, they tend to dry out quickly. Add water-retentive granules to hold moisture in the compost, along with slow-release feed that will help maintain nutrient levels for some time (inset).

Try out the position of the plants while still in their pots to achieve the best juxtaposition of forms and colours. Check that the root mass of your plants will fit into the relatively narrow confines of the container with enough room for soil to surround them by several centimetres in all directions.

Place the plants in the window box and back-fill with more compost until the soil level is 2–3cm/1–1¼in below the rim. When watering, this will ensure that a good pool develops to soak the compost thoroughly.

> **TIP** If you are planting bulbs, they can be placed beneath other plants – bury them twice as deep as their height. Plant spring bulbs such as daffodils and crocus in autumn to early winter and summer bulbs like lilies in late spring.

2

3

Mulching

The purpose of a 5-10cm/2-4in mulching layer around the base of a plant is threefold. The mulch retains moisture in the soil by slowing down evaporation. It also keeps weeds at bay by smothering any dormant seeds or sprouted seedlings. And, where taste dictates, it makes a backdrop that shows off the particular qualities of the plant. There are many types of mulching material available; some you can make yourself and others you will have to buy.

Organic mulches

These need to be applied annually as they break down over time. However, they do in the process feed the soil and improve its structure. Manure and garden compost, which can be home-made (see pages 142–3), certainly improve soil fertility and are particularly useful to vegetable gardeners. They also keeps weeds at bay and retain moisture. Shredded bark, moss, leaf mould and other such fibrous mulches are mostly used around shrubs and trees. They will rot down slowly and have a natural appearance if used judiciously.

Inorganic mulches

Pebbles, shingle, slate and other such inorganic materials do not rot down, so only one application is needed. To ensure that weeds do not appear among them, place a layer of the mulching material over a weedproof fabric 'membrane' that will allow moisture through while preventing unwanted growth. Cut planting holes into the membrane where required. Some inorganic mulches can have a decorative appearance that may suit a particular garden style, and will help dry-garden plants in a cool-climate garden by reflecting heat on to them.

The decorative quality of many modern mulching materials in fact often overrides any functional requirement. It is not unusual to see small coloured mosaic tiles or shells covering the soil at the feet of plants in beds and containers. Glass marbles, coloured ground glass or even chrome ball-bearings can make a striking contemporary backdrop for your plants. In some cases the mulching material itself becomes the focus of the garden, with a few plants interspersed within it to add contrast. Inorganic mulches really open the door to garden decoration, so have fun with innovative materials and make some discoveries of your own.

Mushroom compost, a by-product of the mushroom-growing industry, can be deliverd loose or bought in bags in a garden centre. It is relatively bulky and more suitable for beds than containers.

Mulches like slate can be used to great effect in contrast with bark or to set off foliage. Here smoothed pieces of broken slate enhance the stark white stems of a birch.

Bulky, irregular mulches like manure and garden compost are used for practical purposes in beds rather than as an aesthetic mulch for a container.

Like gravel or slate, white marble pebbles are used more for aesthetic effect than function. Because of their self-compacting nature, a regular 5cm/2in layer is easily achieved, making it suitable for containers. These pebbles can be bought at stone merchants.

mushroom

slate

pebbles

manure

Watering and feeding

Ideally, you should water plants in the cool of the evening and early morning so that there is minimal wastage through evaporation. Make sure you always water for long enough to saturate plant roots and be effective. How often you water your garden depends on the type of soil. If you have light, free-draining soil, water will run through it quickly, leaving plants thirsty, whereas a heavy clay soil may hold water for some time. One way to check that you are providing enough water is to place a jar or cup among the plants and water until about 2cm/1in of water has collected in it; by then the plants should have received enough.

Watering by can

Watering cans are ideal for accurate watering among pots and beds containing seedlings and plants with delicate foliage as well as for reaching window boxes and containers in confined spaces.

Of the different heads available, the most useful is a rose fitting which creates a gentle shower of water that will not erode soil or expose plant roots.

Watering by hose

A hosepipe is ideal for getting water to a multitude of different areas and levels in a garden. Different jet-controlling water guns can be clipped on to the end of a hose to provide the right stream of water for the job in hand. Clipping on a sprinkler is a way to save time when watering a large area like a lawn or a bed. Do not leave a sprinkler unattended as it can result in wastage and waterlogging.

When watering with a hose, ensure that it does not get dragged across the corner of a bed and damage delicate stems. When not in use, store a hose out of the way on a wall-mounted reel.

Lay a 'leaky' irrigation pipe on the soil surface or hide it under a loose layer of mulch or ground-cover planting (left). Sprinklers can be clipped on to the end of a hose; their adjustable nozzles direct water across a specific area (right).

Irrigation systems

After the initial outlay, a simple irrigation system involves economy of both water and effort. A small computerized valve connects to a tap and allows water to flow through 'leaky' (perforated) pipes or sprinkler jets, activated and controlled by a timer that opens and closes the valve at pre-set times. Spray nozzles allow you to target specific thirsty trees or shrubs. The timer can be set to water at night when it will be most effective.

Feeding

Most gardens bring together a variety of plants in quite cramped conditions which can often drain the soil of available nutrients. We have to make allowance for this by providing food at the right time. The three vital nutrients required by plants are: nitrogen for shoots and leaf growth; phosphorus for root growth and germination; potash for flowers and fruit (including tomatoes and potatoes). Apply by one of the following methods.

Manure or garden compost

Bulky organic materials condition the soil while releasing nutrients. Compost needs time to rot down within the soil first, so is often applied in late autumn to be ready the following spring. Manure and home-made compost may come free, or at little expense, and are a key part of good organic practice. Owing to their bulk and irregular composition, it can be difficult to apply such a food source with any great degree of accuracy or to guarantee exactly when nutrients will become available.

Fertilizers

Fertilizers are an effective and accurately measured source of plant food, particularly geared towards plants with a high yield – say vegetables, fruit or roses. Organic fertilizers, such as fish, blood and bonemeal, have a more readily available mix of the

Organic materials like seaweed, manure, nettles and comfrey are made into liquid feeds and applied to the foliage with a watering can or a hose–end applicator.

key nutrients but they still require the activity of micro-organisms in the soil to break them down. These 'slow-release' organic fertilizers are either added to the soil prior to planting, incorporated at the time of planting or used as a topdressing in an established garden in the spring.

For rapid action, gardeners often turn to artificial fertilizers. These granular, powdered or liquid products come in many forms, with varying compositions of chemical compounds to suit particular plants. Normally added to the soil at planting time, or as an interim feed during a plant's growth, they allow for accuracy in application with the assurance of a rapid uptake of nutrients.

Foliar feeds

Where soil is shallow, access to roots inadequate or a plant is being exhausted due to heavy cropping or ailing due to pest attack or disease, a foliar feed provides a 'quick fix' of nutrients to bolster a plant.

Making compost

The subject of myth and legend in the gardening world, good compost is the 'holy grail' of horticulture and the quest for it can often become fervent. The backbone of any organic garden, making compost is an economical and effective means of recycling a large amount of household and garden waste into a rich source of nutrients that can be returned to the soil as organic matter.

Composting materials

Keep a bucket or bin in your kitchen and throw into it all scraps from fruit and vegetables, along with coffee grounds and teabags. Other foodstuffs can be added but avoid meat, fish and poultry to prevent vermin being attracted to the heap. As your material builds up, add to it waste paper in equal proportion to the volume of plant-based material. Scrunch up newspaper so that it does not form thick layers. Envelopes, egg cartons, toilet roll tubes, kitchen towels and cartons can all be included provided they do not have a plastic or foil lining. It is best to add these ingredients consecutively to achieve a fairly even distribution.

Garden waste such as grass clippings and annual weeds can be put on the heap, but not perennial weeds, for example knotweed and bindweed, that have regenerative roots. Avoid woody prunings and evergreen foliage that will not decompose fast enough. Where you do add a quantity of plant material like grass clippings, balance it with a layer of carboniferous material such as straw or paper to prevent a high build-up of nitrogen in the heap.

Building the heap

You should stack the compost heap in contact with the soil's surface; this makes the composting process more effective as worms, insects and other

scraps...

1

2

3

MAKING COMPOST   **1 4 3**

invertebrates that will assist in breaking down the mix have greater access to it. Where space is plentiful – and appearance is not too important – you can make a broad heap with a large surface area in direct contact with the soil. In a smaller garden, a tidy heap approximately one metre square will work well. Retain the heap with some form of enclosure; this is commonly made from a framework of chicken wire, from railway sleepers or stacked straw bales, or you can use a ready-made slatted timber bin.

Generally, a heap is filled over the course of a year, from spring to winter, until it is about 1m/3ft 3in high, then it remains sealed until it is required in the garden. To speed the process, sprinkle garden lime on the heap each time you empty your bin on to it. Add a layer of well-rotted manure every so often to stimulate activity in the upper levels.

Make sure that the compost heap does not dry out; you may need to wet any paper that goes into the heap if it shows a tendency to dry out. Keep the heap well insulated with a lid or a piece of old carpet to maintain a high temperature inside. This will speed up the process of decomposition as well as ensuring that all the weed seeds in the heap are completely neutralized.

Two bins are often placed side by side as this allows for one to be filled while the contents of the other, which rotted down throughout the year in which it was assembled, are slowly redistributed around the garden.

Wormeries

Ready-made worm bins are available from mail-order suppliers who advertise in the back pages of gardening magazines. In a wormery, a colony of tiger worms slowly eats its way through compost as it is added, leaving beneath it excreted and decomposed compost ready for garden use. A wormery is fun for children to watch; it can even be kept in the kitchen.

compost

The best thing about home-made compost is that so little goes to waste from the kitchen.

You will be amazed at how much waste material it takes to fill a compost bin. As the layers decompose and compact, so the level in the bin continually drops. Placing a lid on top will insulate the heap and speed up decomposition.

From bucket to spade in only twelve months, kitchen waste is turned into a rich, friable soil mix.

Training climbers

In the artificial environment of a garden, climbing plants need to be trained and given support. As these plants are grown for show, they are usually trained against walls, over structures and supports or through trees and shrubs so that their blooms and foliage can be seen to best effect. Woody climbers such as roses and wisteria are often tied to training wires to hold them against a wall or fence, to keep their growth manageable and take full advantage of the vertical space. Alternatively, trellis panels can be fixed to a wall with the posts against the wall and plants trained up the front.

The means of supporting climbers can often be decorative in themselves. Structures like pergolas, arbours, trellis and arches are often placed in a garden to make a stylish frame for the embellishment of flowering and scented climbing plants. Such structures need not always be formal and highly finished – a few hazel rods bent into a shape while still supple can make a simple but attractive framework in a bed or container.

A variety of plant supports: a home-made frame of hazel allows morning glories to weave a flowering globe (left); a rustic trellis above a fence tempts a honeysuckle (top right); a wisteria twines through a pergola which provides enough structure for stems to find their own way (bottom right).

Fixing wires

Drill a hole in sound brickwork and place in it a rawlplug, then screw in a sturdy vine eye. You will need several vine eyes to maintain tension on a wire over 2m/6ft 6in long.

Fix a length of galvanized wire through one vine eye and attach it with tension to the next vine eye. Space the wires 30–45cm/12–18in apart to allow enough room between the trained stems of the climber.

Using adjustable ties, secure the plant's new growth to the wire as it develops during the growing season. Check these ties every year and loosen them off as the stems thicken. The vine eyes ensure that the wires are held sufficiently clear of the wall for air to circulate.

Pruning

In the wild, plants are 'pruned' through grazing and extremes of winter weather that remove soft growth from their sturdier framework; the plant puts this growth back on the next season. So pruning is not a gardener's artifice but an essential part of the natural rejuvenation process many trees and shrubs undergo. Like many 'technical' areas of gardening, pruning has become something of a science in itself with considerable, often daunting, complexity. You will not go far wrong if you follow basic principles.

Equipment Ensure you have a good pair of sharp secateurs, a pruning saw and a pair of loppers. For thorny plants you may need a thick pair of gloves.
General pruning The main purpose of pruning is to keep trees and shrubs free from dead and diseased stems and to maintain a good profile within a bed. First cut out any dead or diseased growth so that you are considering only the plant's living structure. Make all your pruning cuts above a leaf bud or joint. After carrying out any major pruning, mulch heavily or feed the plant to compensate for the temporary loss of vigour.

Basic one-third prune

A mess of crowded stems on this viburnum is depriving the plant of light and air.

Cut back to the base a third of the stems, choosing the oldest and thickest. Use a pruning saw if you cannot get secateurs into the centre.

Make all your cuts just above a leaf bud or joint and angle them slightly to prevent rainwater soaking into the healing stem.

Trim back the remaining stems by a third to a half, using loppers or, for the lighter stems, secateurs.

Now that light and air can reach the centre of the rejuvenated shrub, the weaker stems will thicken up and put on more vigorous growth, leading to the production of larger leaves and blooms.

The one-third prune This basic method of formative pruning (see below left) encourages vigorous flowering and strong leaf growth. Use it as a one-off treament to rein in a wayward specimen or as a means of continued rejuvenation every year for mature shrub roses and deciduous and evergreen shrubs like *Choisya ternata* and *Viburnum opulus*. In spring, add up the total number of main stems and remove a third of them to ground level. Cut out any weak and crossing growth and trim back the remaining older stems by a third to a half.

Hard pruning Hard pruning improves flowering on vigorous deciduous shrubs like buddleja and caryopteris. As the buds swell in early spring, cut all growth back to a strong bud at the woody base of the plant 15–30cm/ 6–12in from ground level. The plant will respond with strong new growth as the season proceeds.

Cutting back to base This encourages the production of strong stems in the winter months on trees and shrubs grown for their colourful bark.

Cutting back to base

1 In mid– to late spring, using sharp secateurs, cut back all growth on trees and shrubs like willow and cornus that are grown for their colourful bark.

2 Cut shrubs back to ground level (known as coppicing), as shown above or, in the case of trees, to within a couple of buds from the main stem (known as pollarding).

Pruning a climbing rose

This method suits vigorous climbers and ramblers over three years old. Prune each autumn, after flowering, or once in three years, depending on its vigour.

1 This tangled rose (right) has become overcrowded and has ceased to flower profusely.

2 Wearing gloves and using sharp secateurs, remove to ground level up to a third of stems, selecting thick, woody ones. Cut back all long, trailing stems that flowered by up to a half.

3 With the plant thinned you can see which stems to tie in.

Sowing seed

Sowing in trays

This method is often used to get plants started early in the season, especially to fill containers and window boxes.

Fill a seed tray with a suitable potting compost and firm the top with a board. Sow seeds thinly on the surface and scatter compost to cover them. Write plant details and date of sowing on a plant tag and label the tray.

Water in the seeds gently, using a watering can with a rose attachment – be careful not to wash them away. Place in a light, frost-free place until the seeds germinate.

When seedlings of a manageable size appear, lift them gently by a leaf, never the stem, and prick out into pots or modules.

As the seedlings get more sturdy, continue potting on, increasing the size of pot as the plants develop.

When they are sufficiently well grown to be handled, transplant into individual pots. Harden plants off slowly in a cold frame before planting outside.

Sowing outside

Prepare the soil by raking it to a fine tilth (see page 132), then firm the surface with the flat of the rake.

If planting vegetables, make a narrow, shallow drill with a trowel and sow seeds thinly, remembering to date and label each row. If you are planting flowering annuals in a bed, simply sprinkle the seeds on the surface and rake over a light covering of soil. Make a note of the area covered so you leave it undisturbed.

Depending on what you have planted, you may need to thin out seedlings as they grow. Follow the instructions on the packet.

1

2

Simple propagation

Plants should not be seen as one-offs in a garden. With a little light surgery, some coaxing and loving care they can produce generations of siblings to crowd your beds and borders and maintain a perpetual presence in your garden through the years. If you can spare the time to carry out some of the following procedures you will not only ensure continued vigour within the planted areas of your garden but may also create replacements for potential losses due to old age or accidental damage as well as generating spare plants to swap with fellow gardeners. Where propagation gets complex and scientific, I tend to avoid it, but the simple processes of taking softwood and semi-ripe cuttings and dividing perennials should enable you to get creative with a wide variety of your plants without having to put on a white coat.

Taking softwood cuttings (top row)

This method is suitable for herbaceous perennials like phlox, achillea, campanula, delphinium, sedum and salvia. Equipment needed: a cuttings knife, horticultural washed sand, potting compost, pots, clear polythene bag, twigs or spills and plant tags.

1 In spring, when the shoots of perennials are still soft and sappy, take 5–7cm/2–3in cuttings of vigorous new growth, ending in a strong leaf bud. Remove the lower leaves and trim the stem sharply just beneath a leaf joint.

2 Insert the cuttings into a container filled with sandy compost and water well. Place in a light position with a constant temperature of 16–24°C/60–75°F.

3 Leave the pot on a window sill inside a polythene bag (kept apart with twigs or spills) or use a heated propagator. Pot cuttings on individually into potting compost as soon as they have rooted.

Taking semi-ripe cuttings (middle row)

This method can be used on most shrubby plants, including climbers.

1 In late summer take 10–15cm/4–6in cuttings from side shoots or the tip of main shoots; pull off the lower leaves. Cut the stem to just below a leaf joint. If the plant has large leaves, cut them in half to make space in the pot for the cuttings and to reduce water loss.

2 Dip the cutting in a hormone rooting powder and insert it into a container so that the tip of its base enters soil or compost through a 3cm/1in layer of sharp sand.

3 Place several cuttings around the outside of the container, then water well and place the container in a shaded frost-free environment such as a cold frame. Pot on the cuttings individually once they have rooted.

Dividing perennials and bulbs (bottom row)

In time, perennials grow to form dense clumps that, if left undivided, will begin to thin out at the centre as they become congested. Once you divide the clumps in spring, they will rejuvenate and grow faster, as well as providing numerous smaller plants to spread around a garden or offer to friends.

1 In spring, as new shoots start to show, lift the plant clump, with its root mass, using a spade. Shake off any excess soil, then place it on the ground.

2 Prise apart the clump and discard its old centre. If the plant has fibrous roots you may need to use two forks back to back to open up the clump. If it has fleshy roots, use a knife to cut through it.

3 Separate out the smaller clumps of young healthy roots, tubers or bulbs taken from the outer edges and trim the foliage. Replant the new clumps.

> T I P Lift plants like iris, that have rhizomes, in late summer. Cut off the swollen younger sections that show strong roots and shoots and replant, with the rhizome just showing at ground level.

Garden tools

The hard work involved in making a garden can become less arduous if you have the right tools. Investing in a sturdy set of tools will prevent tasks being left half-completed owing to a lack of the right equipment or frustration at unnecessarily slow progress. It is best to shop for tools at an outlet that stocks a wide range of different brands so that you can compare several versions of the same tool. Look for simple, robust design: gadgets are always no more than gadgets and, in my experience, inevitably end up gathering cobwebs. All tools should feel comfortable and manageable in use. Digging tools such as spades and forks should be well balanced – try flexing them to see that all joints are strong and will stand up to garden use. The following selection will cater for the basic needs of most gardens.

Spades   It is worth having two spades: a digging spade for major tasks such as breaking up large areas of soil, digging planting holes for trees and shrubs and working manure into empty beds, and a smaller border spade for more confined tasks like planting perennials.

Forks   As with spades, two forks are useful. Use a sturdy digging fork to break up large clods of earth when creating new beds and getting pernicious roots out of the ground, and a smaller digging fork for weeding between plants in beds and for cultivating smaller areas.

Garden rake   Useful for levelling soil in preparation for seeding or laying turf: a compact head with large tines makes raking an expanse of soil easier and faster than with a rake with a larger head. Rakes are

In addition to garden spades and forks you will need an edging tool (turfing iron), a Dutch hoe and a garden rake (right). Pruning and cutting tools (below) include, from bottom to top: secateurs, loppers, garden shears and pruning saw.

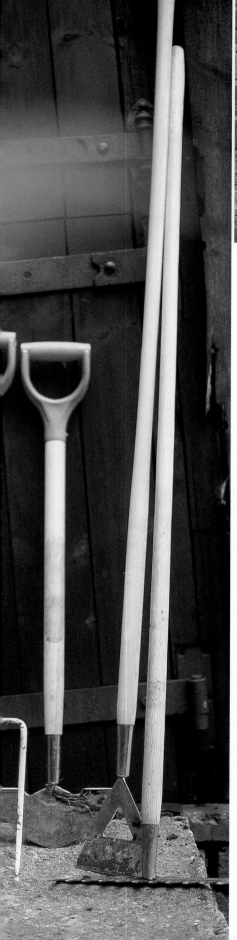

A hosepipe is most conveniently stored on a wall-mounted reel (above left). For planting in containers useful hand tools include a trowel and fork, a bulb planter with measured depths and a dibber for bulbs and seedlings (above right).

also handy when preparing vegetable beds before planting.

Dutch hoe The ideal tool for cultivating in beds between plants, a lightweight hoe with a long handle deals swiftly with seedling weeds over a large area. The blade severs foliage from roots when pushed through the soil and uproots weeds when drawn back towards you.

Edging tool Ideal for cutting shapes in turf before making a new bed and for tidying lawn edges to maintain the definition of a bed.

Loppers Used for trimming small branches on trees and shrubs.

Secateurs Specially made for pruning the stems of climbers and shrubs. Look for a pair with a sharp, solid cutting blade and a smooth action for efficient cutting without tearing.

Cuttings knife Used for taking cuttings from shrubs and perennials. Choose a knife that fits comfortably into the palm of your hand so you can maintain a firm grip. A sharp flat cutting edge is essential.

Shears Used primarily for hedge cutting and topiary work. Make sure you choose shears that are strong but lightweight.

Sheep shears One-handed sheep shears are a useful additional tool for clipping intricate and smaller topiary pieces.

Pruning saw For cutting out large stems in confined spaces such as at the base of a mature shrub where loppers cannot be used.

Hand trowel and fork For planting bedding plants and small perennials and working in containers, such as window boxes.

Bulb planter These often come with measurements on the side to aid correct depth in bulb planting. Narrow blade allows for planting close to other bulbs and plants without too much disruption.

Dibber For planting bulbs and seedling plants.

Troubleshooting

As the plants in your garden start to grow and prosper, they will inevitably come under attack from various pests and diseases. This attack can be minimal and fleeting or it can be considerable and alarming, especially when all that you have striven for suddenly ends up on something else's menu. There is no guaranteed way to prevent pests or diseases from affecting your plants and the range of products available to deal with them indicates how seriously gardeners take this threat.

There is a temptation to attack at the first sign of trouble, often by using a chemically based product that has a reassuringly dramatic sounding list of active ingredients – but this can cause harm well beyond the individual perpetrator you are targeting. Prevention is always better than cure, and a great deal can be done to prepare a garden for the inevitable onslaught of pests and diseases so it can sustain any damage that occurs and go on to survive it. Bear in mind that gardens are part of the natural world and plants are a source of food and habitat for a great many insects and animals, so some losses must be tolerated. But keep them to a minimum by making sure your garden receives the best attention. If you are vigilant, you can get to grips with an infestation or attack in its early stages and reduce the potential for it to cause long-term damage to your plants.

Good housekeeping
• Keep your garden clear of debris and rubbish like large piles of leaves, stacks of bricks and broken pots that can harbour pests like slugs and snails.
• A well-nourished soil contains plenty of nutrients that will foster strong, healthy plants with good immunity, resistant to attack, so improve it regularly with additions of organic matter.
• All plants should be fed, pruned and watered as necessary, to ensure they grow strongly.
• Where possible, avoid monocultures (high concentrations of just one type of plant) as there is a greater chance for specific problems to build up, such as aphids, or spores of black spot fungus in a rose garden. If you do plant roses in high concentrations, underplant with a variety of herbaceous plants that will flower before and after the roses are at their best.

Some of the main offenders and some of the gardener's allies are described below.

Garden menaces

Slugs and snails
Slugs and snails hide by day in cool, moist shady places such as beneath pots, in long grass or stacks of bricks. They then emerge in the cool of the evening to feast on the lush new foliage of mature and seedling plants, especially perennials, annual bedding plants and vegetables. Damage is worst in the spring when plants are just showing their new leaves and are most susceptible to being weakened by attack. Large chunks removed from the edge of leaves or whole seedlings disappearing overnight to be replaced by glistening film-like trails are signs of these voracious nocturnal feeders.

Where possible, protect lush foliage plants such as hostas in pots. A ring of ash, coarse sharp sand or any other gritty or rough material around the base of plants will dissuade the majority of these pests – but there will always be a few dare-devils that are not intimidated by a scratchy belly! Remove any lower leaves that touch the ground, making effective slug ramps, and cut away any foliage around the edge of beds that might harbour slugs or snails. To assess the problem, go out at night with a torch and collect the numbers that will have arrived in your garden – they can be thrown against a hard paved surface as breakfast for the birds or killed just as quickly with boiling water. Where your planting is confined in raised beds, nematodes will keep slug and snail numbers in check for several months per dose.

Perhaps one of the most demonized of garden pests, the slug is a voracious devourer of soft, juicy foliage and tender stems, especially on new growth.

Aphids

There are hundreds of different species of aphid, including blackfly (see pages 158–9), that attack and live upon plants. They suck the sap from growing tips, thus weakening plants, spread viral infections and secrete a honeydew that blocks plant pores and soon spawns grey sooty moulds. If you catch infestations early enough you can greatly reduce their numbers by rubbing them off young shoots with your fingers, or spraying them off with a jet of water. For larger colonies, repeated spraying with a soapy water solution will deplete numbers as it breaks down their protective waxy coating.

Caterpillars

Found chomping holes in leaves from late spring to early autumn, caterpillars are particularly fond of brassicas in the vegetable garden. These larvae come in all shapes and sizes and feed at an alarming rate. Check your plants regularly as they develop and crush any eggs you spot on the underside of leaves as well as picking off caterpillars by hand; put them on the bird table or dispose of them as you see fit. In an ordered vegetable garden crops can be protected under fleece or fine netting. Don't be obsessive about this – the odd caterpillar won't be too harmful – and remember they are only a stage in the development of increasingly rare moths and butterflies.

Vine weevils

A hidden terror beneath the soil, especially in pots, vine weevil larvae eat roots and slowly weaken a plant. Unless you spot them when repotting, the first sign of their presence will be a plant that seems to give no response to watering or feeding and slowly starts to wilt, by which time it is already too late. Another candidate for the bird table, the white maggot-like grubs – that can number in the hundreds per pot – are about 1cm/½in long with brown heads. The adults, which take crescent-shaped cuts from the edges of leaves, are armour-clad small beetles with two long antennae, that are capable of laying over one thousand eggs.

Control is not always effective. There are some potent products containing Imidacloprid if you want to go for chemical warfare, but a nematode that preys on vine-weevil grubs is now available as a biological control. This can be purchased through mail order and is applied in late summer.

Always check plants when repotting. Once you have identified an outbreak, throw out all contaminated soil and make sure you do not recycle compost from any of these pots. Renew the pots with an insecticide-treated compost for all but food plants. Standing pots on blocks in water or putting a grease band around the edge of a pot may deter the flightless adults.

Predatory allies

If you have the patience to wait, predators will appear hot on the heels of an outbreak of garden pests and will begin to devour slugs, aphids and caterpillars with gusto.

Ladybirds and their larvae

The ladybird is probably the best loved of garden insects and its reputation is well deserved, thanks to the savage and destructive appetite of its larval stage. Though adult ladybirds consume aphids too, it is their larvae that do the real damage, each one eating hundreds of fully mature aphids. Allow a few nettles to grow in your garden and they will attract ladybirds early in the season in pursuit of nettle aphids. This will ensure an army of the small, elongated segmented larvae, recognizable by four yellow markings on their flanks, that will tear into your aphid population.

Hoverflies and their larvae

Hoverflies look like flattened wasps and hang in the air making a high-pitched whirring sound. The baggy grub-like larvae, buff green with black and white longitudinal stripes, also feed voraciously on aphids. Hoverflies are attracted to the garden by open-faced flowers such as calendula and limnanthes, from which they extract nectar.

Lacewings and their larvae

Adult lacewings are delicate-looking green insects with long antennae and four transparent lacy wings. The larva, which is covered in clusters of short spiky hairs and is about four times the length of an aphid, has an appetite to match that of the ladybird. Attract them to the garden by planting flowers among your vegetables.

Birds

From blue tits to barn owls, all birds will take garden pests. The smaller songbirds are deft at dealing with slugs, aphids, grubs and caterpillars, so place bird tables around the garden and leave the seedheads on plants in the autumn. Hanging out fat and nuts in winter will encourage tits, wrens and robins to seek out overwintering insects that are tucked into cracks in bark and other hiding places. If you have cats, make sure they have bells on their collars to keep bird fatalities to a minimum and encourage nesting by putting up bird boxes.

Frogs

Where you have water in your garden there is the chance that frogs and toads may appear. These amphibians will make great headway into slug and snail populations. Make sure pools or ponds have flattish rocks at the edge so that frogs and toads can crawl in and out of the water relatively easily.

Second only to the robin as a gardener's friend, the ladybird wages its own campaign against sap-sucking aphids.

Fighting disease

There are many air-borne and soil-borne diseases simply waiting for the appearance of pristine leaves and stems. The most common are listed below, along with a description of their symptoms and the best means of treating them.

Powdery mildew

This white powdery coating appears on the leaves and stems of vegetables, fruit and herbaceous plants, often causing foliage to yellow and wilt. It commonly affects plants that are suffering from a lack of water in hot and dry conditions. Powdery mildew also strikes plants that are crowded together in cramped conditions. To prevent an outbreak, ensure plants are watered well and given plenty of space, especially when grown in thin, free-draining soil. Where an outbreak does occur, remove affected plants or spray foliage with a product that contains sulfur.

Black spot

Specific to roses, this fungus produces dark spots with a yellow halo on the older leaves. This can spread across the whole plant to the extent that it becomes entirely defoliated. Black spot overwinters on dead leaves that have fallen to the ground and is a particular threat to the monoculture of a rose garden. To reduce the risk of an outbreak, collect and burn all prunings and mulch heavily around the plants so that the spores remain locked into the soil. Underplant your roses with herbaceous perennials and plant garlic, said to inhibit a build-up of black spot spores in the soil nearby. In severe cases gardeners use a proprietary fungicide.

Rust

Tiny orange spots appear on the underside of leaves which cause a yellow discoloration to the upper side. This can cause the leaves to dry out and fall prematurely, weakening the plant. As with black spot, remove all fallen leaves and prunings and cut out any stems that appear to be affected. Fungicide is again a last resort.

Honey fungus

The scourge of woody plants such as trees and shrubs, this fungus attacks struggling plants and administers the *coup de grâce* – often very quickly. It is only noticeable in autumn when the honey-coloured toadstools appear above ground around the base of the infected plant. If you look beneath the bark you will see a white matted mycelium and/or black bootlace strands known to mycologists as rhizomorphs. Affected plants only partially come into leaf, wilt or die back. There are chemical products to control honey fungus but they can involve the use of quite unpleasant ingredients. Remove as much as you can of an infected plant's trunk and root mass from your garden and wait a year before planting any new trees and shrubs. Bury a ring of heavy-duty polythene to a depth of at least 60cm/2ft to prevent any returning fungus from getting in. Alternatively, develop a taste for the toadstools themselves which the Italians prize quite highly.

The appearance of a powdery white dusting of mildew (opposite, top), if untreated, will cause foliage to drop and fruit to fail.
Scourge of the vegetable garden, blackfly (opposite, bottom left) increase their numbers rapidly on the stems and leaves of developing beans, spinach and beetroot. As well as consuming valuable plant nutrients, blackfly can be a vector for fungal infections.
Black spot (opposite, bottom right) is a common fungal disease associated with roses which, if not controlled, can defoliate entire plants.

Eradicating weeds

In spring, when your herbaceous plants are putting on new growth, perennial and annual weeds are doing just the same. There are usually a far greater quantity of weed seeds and seedlings lurking within your soil than the numbers of plants that you have put in – and they are normally plants that grow very quickly indeed. Weeds can be controlled before things get out of hand:

• Dig any new beds thoroughly and leave to lie fallow for a month in the growing season, then remove any remaining weeds that show themselves.
• A thick mulching layer on beds in autumn, with a top-up in spring, will suppress weeds by keeping their seeds buried and dormant.
• Ground-cover plants or a mixed underplanting will help crowd weeds out before they take hold.

Capable of breaking through concrete and asphalt, Japanese knotweed should be eradicated at the first sign of entry into your garden.

Bindweed rapidly twines itself around other plants, cutting out light and eventually overcoming them; it is seen here strangling the stems of lavender.

- If weeds persist after this, then a regular hoe, as seedling weeds appear between your plants, will severely knock them back. It is important to do this weekly in spring or you will miss your chance and the weeds will get established, making control more time-consuming. There are, however, a few menaces that need more severe measures.

Japanese knotweed
Imported by the Victorians as an ornamental marginal plant for ponds and river banks, this has become a threat in town and countryside alike. Growing to 3m/10ft tall, it forms dense thickets and spreads by means of tough, persistent underground stems that are almost impossible to dig out entirely – any fragment left behind will simply regrow. The only way to deal with an invasion of this plant is to allow it to develop soft, leafy growth, then carefully apply a product containing glyphosate on a regular basis. If your neighbour has Japanese knotweed and it hasn't already entered your garden under the fence, consider burying a heavy-duty polythene barrier to a depth of at least 60cm/2ft.

Bindweed
This perennial climber spreads rapidly through the soil, with any root fragment left behind after uprooting sure to regrow. If you can remove all growth down to just below ground level on a weekly basis you will gradually weaken the plant until its root system shrivels and dies. Alternatively, encourage bindweed to coil itself around a specially placed cane so that the foliage is not in contact with other plants. When it has reached approximately 1m/3ft 3in in height, paint the leaves with a systemic weedkiller that will cause the plant to die back throughout its entire root system.

Ground elder
This low perennial weed spreads through seed and creeping rhizomes in the top 10–20cm/4–8in of soil. Once it has infiltrated an established bed, it can be extremely difficult to eradicate – so deal with it the minute you see it. You must remove every fragment of the root or it will regrow. It is said that it can take seven years entirely to remove ground elder from the soil by hand, but don't be dissuaded by this – keep ripping up the foliage on a regular basis and it will eventually give up. If the invasion is too severe and you have not the time to cover the soil with a suffocating layer of carpet for several months, then apply a systemic weedkiller.

Nettles
Stinging nettles spread through a mass of shallow yellow roots. When cut back to just above this root mass, they will regenerate, so if you aim to eradicate them you must either dig them up, scalp them (cutting the stems right back to the crown of the root mass) or hire a gas burner and burn them off. Alternatively, you could eat them – young nettle tops make a delicious soup and a very refreshing tea.

Dandelions
Though many people tolerate them, dandelions are a common problem in lawns, where regular mowing makes them grow as mat-like, ground-hugging rosettes of leaves. As dandelions cannot easily be plucked and destroyed, the taproot – which may be up to 20cm/8in long – must be dug out or a treatment of systemic weedkiller applied.

Annual weeds
Annual weeds such as chickweed, groundsel and fat hen are fast growers. Though they do not represent such an obstinate garden presence as the perennial weeds, they self-seed prolifically and should be hoed off more than once a week.

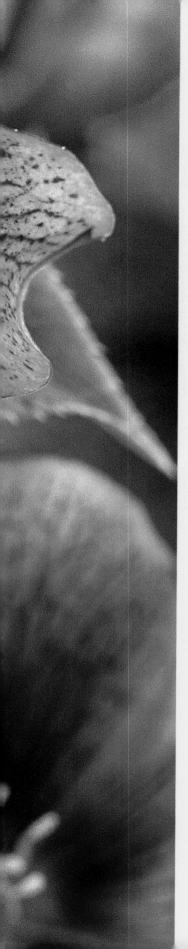

plant manifesto

Plants are the unifying essence of gardens – the vital living force that flows through and around the structural elements that demarcate and divide our outdoor environment. By integrating such static features as walls, seating, terraces and buildings with nature's sprawling energy, plants enable us to make vibrant living spaces.

Gardeners choose their plants from books, mail-order catalogues, nurseries, visits to public gardens and those of friends. As our gardens develop, so our experience increases and we come across different plants and new combinations to introduce to beds and borders. It takes time to assemble a list of plants that will work together. The picture is best built up slowly, (see pages 124–5) with planting implemented in phases from the large, structural elements such as trees and evergreen shrubs down to the smallest herb for a gap between paving.

With a whole world of plants to choose from, here are some exciting, inspirational and easy-to-grow starting points, which are all readily available. I have chosen to focus on categories of plants that are important in establishing beautiful and satisfying garden pictures all year round. It is usually easy to fill a garden with colour in high summer. However, it is not so easy to plan for architectural effects, to ensure you have a constant background of attractive foliage, to fill that tired late-summer gap, or to plan for interest in spring, so these are some of the categories I've included.

Spring interest

Often the most appreciated of plants – arriving after the long monochromatic months of winter – spring flowers start a new cycle as they push through warming soil and emerge from fresh green leaves.

Anemone nemorosa

In their native environment, wood anemones form densely colonizing perennial mats of low-growing, divided foliage that appear in spring and will carpet a woodland floor where soil is moist, rich and well drained. Seek a partially shaded site in your garden and allow the small, simple white flowers to scramble around the base of developing perennials and the stems of trees and shrubs from spring into early summer.

Anthriscus sylvestris

A perennial beauty that seeds itself in meadows and along hedges, roadsides and river banks, cow parsley's appearance brings grace and naturalness to a garden. These qualities can enhance the showier appearance of more cultivated blooms when *A. sylvestris* infiltrates a herbaceous border, and can add texture to a wilder, more natural look when combined with foxgloves, verbascums and campanulas. Umbels of minuscule white flowers are supported on narrow stems 90cm/3ft tall above a mass of lacy foliage. *A. sylvestris* 'Ravenswing' has deep purplish brown leaves and stems.

Aquilegia

The columbine's small, exotic-looking flared trumpets are drawn delicately forward from long thin spurs and held proudly on delicate stems up to 90cm/3ft tall in sun or partial shade in late spring. This perennial offers a great range of colours from blues, deep violets and crimson to pinks, yellows and whites. Once you have planted a few

different varieties, all manner of colour combinations will arise as the plants interbreed and self-seed – perfect for a carefree garden. *A. atrata* has a brooding presence with the darkest of purples, while *A. vulgaris* 'Nora Barlow' has showy, almost dahlia-like spurless flowers of red, pink and green petals.

Crocus vernus

Top of the menu for all squirrels and top of the list for early spring bulbs, the Dutch crocus is a native of grasslands and open woodland which makes it ideal for planting beneath trees or in meadows and lawns where the grass is left to grow a little longer. Some prefer to throw them across the grass or border and plant them where they land; others group them in clumps and patterns. Wherever you plant them, their white, lilac and purple hoards will increase. To deter squirrels, lay 2.5cm/1in mesh over bulbs planted 8cm/3in deep in soil that is not too rich.

Dicentra spectabilis

Known as bleeding heart on account of its heart-shaped flowers that hang in pendulous racemes, rising through and sometimes concealed within layers of fresh green foliage. The 1.25cm/½in long flowers look like plump little seedpods; each 'bleeds' a single droplet (the white inner petals) that highlights the rich pink colour of the outer petals. Ideal in a woodland garden or a mixed border, it is very hardy and will grow to 1.2m/4ft if planted in a partially shaded position in rich soil – though it will tolerate sunshine in a soil that retains some moisture.

Erythronium dens-canis

The dog's-tooth violet inhabits open woodland and mountainous grasslands where its lustrous purple-dappled green leaves are a striking feature in themselves against the sepia and monochrome tones of dead leaves and rocks. The foliage is accompanied, in late spring, by flowers on 15cm/6in stems, that seem almost to be bending their heads as if in a gale. The pink outer petals are pulled back behind the flower, away from the protruding purple anthers. Plant bulbs in the autumn 15cm/6in deep in rich, well-drained soil in partial shade.

Euphorbia amygdaloides var. robbiae

An invasive and spreading hardy perennial that can happily deal with one of the more challenging planting situations that gardeners face – that of dry shade. Very dark green leathery leaves surround the lower part of the upright 45cm/18in stems in whorls. From early spring to midsummer tiny lime-green, saucer-shaped flowers open in cymes on 18cm/7in extensions of the leaf stems. This euphorbia has a slightly alien look to it when in flower, but is a great companion to the dusty blue flowers of *Brunnera macrophylla* and purple-flowered hellebores.

Fritillaria meleagris

A 30cm/12in beacon of beauty in the spring garden, when bare soil might otherwise dull the senses, snake's-head fritillaries – whose flowers range from white to dark purple in colour – are perfection in miniature. The pale purple is most captivating as the petals of the drooping, bell-shaped 5cm/2in flowerheads are tessellated with a chequerboard of light and darker squares. In the wild, snake's-head fritillaries are found in the flood plains of rivers and damp meadows where they can mass together in high numbers. Plant the bulbs at three to four times their own depth in autumn, in sun or shade.

Dicentra spectabilis

Fritillaria meleagris

Pulmonaria 'Mawson's Blue'

Galanthus elwesii

Galanthus

From winter into spring, the bulbs of snowdrops push out strap-like, deep green leaves with a grey sheen that surround a flowering stem up to 20cm/8in tall; this produces delicate honey-scented white flowers with green-flecked centres. A great number of garden forms and hybrids are available from bulb catalogues. Snowdrops are best planted 'in the green' – as sprouted bulbs – and will increase to form large clumps. They are reliably hardy and favour a rich, well-drained soil in partial or deep shade. They will look stunning at the base of a white-stemmed *Betula utilis* var. *jacquemontii*.

Helleborus x hybridus

Hellebores, or Lenten roses, flower in early spring and offer a variety of different flower forms, ranging from white, through pink to purple and as near to black as you can get. The dark

green leathery leaves, that generally persist through winter, are parted by thick 45cm/18in flower stems topped with open-faced waxy flowers that look out across the surrounding bed or nod sheepishly towards the ground. Plant on banks, terraces, raised beds or in pots to enjoy the flowers fully and trim back larger leaves on flowering. A perfect customer for a shady border or a woodland planting. Likes rich, heavy soil.

Hesperis matronalis

At 1.2m/4ft, sweet rocket is a relatively tall-growing hardy perennial that freely self-seeds. A light, informal-looking plant with delicate small, lilac or white 4-petalled flowers that open in panicles from late spring to early summer and release a sweet stock-like scent at dusk to lure pollinating moths. A good companion for shady sedges such as *Luzula sylvatica* and *Carex pendula*, *H. matronalis* can topple a bit

once in flower so may need the support of canes or of other plants in close proximity. Plant in rich, well-drained soil in sun or partial shade and remove seedpods to control its spread if required.

Prunus 'Taihaku'

The great white cherry – and aptly named. One of the most beautiful of all the flowering cherries that grace the coming of spring with their extravagant blossom. This strong-growing, robust deciduous tree up to 8m/25ft tall accompanies the coppery tones of its fresh, unfurling new leaves with large 5cm/2in dazzling white flowers in clusters in mid-spring. Requires full sun and a moist, well-drained soil.

Pulmonaria

Among the first plants to flower in spring, pulmonarias make very useful ground-cover plants that get well-established before the weeds even know what has smothered them. *P.* 'Mawson's Blue' has rich blue flowers on 35cm/14in stems that enliven shady corners. For the full foliage effect try *P. saccharata* with evergreen 30cm/12in long, coarsely textured mid-green leaves splashed with silver and greenish white blotches, followed by blue and violet flowers in late spring. Likes a moisture-retentive soil.

Syringa vulgaris 'Mme Lemoine'

A profuse flowering variety of common lilac that grows to a height of 7m/22ft, *S. vulgaris* 'Mme Lemoine' bears compact panicles of double white, richly scented spring flowers and is ideal for a small plot or front garden where space is at a premium. Although the flowering period is not very long, the rich shape and scent of the blooms make up for it. Best at the back of a mixed border or planted among other trees and shrubs that will draw attention as the flowers of the lilac fade. Fairly drought-tolerant once established, plant lilac in neutral soil in full sun and cut out suckers and crossing stems in late winter.

Late summer

Late summer in the garden can arrive as a missed opportunity – a lacklustre pause with beds all leaf and seedheads. But there are many beautiful, exciting plants to straddle this gap before autumn arrives.

Kniphofia 'Little Maid'

Aster x frikartii 'Mönch'

The best aster by far, *A. frikartii* 'Mönch' produces a continuum of large lavender-blue flowers up to 6cm/2½ in wide with golden centres above dark green foliage from mid-summer to autumn. The profusion of starry blue flowers that rolls across the foliage at a height of about 1.2m/4ft adds decoration to the linear blades of many ornamental grasses as well as the late-summer flowers of heleniums, sedums and echinaceas. A hardy perennial for a well-drained fertile soil in sun.

Canna

Exotic, tropical show-offs that are fully entitled to a lack of modesty. Canna lilies are large-leaved flowering perennials that will only overwinter outdoors in the warmest of climates. They are often planted in pots and taken indoors in winter, or lifted from beds in late autumn and stored till spring. Cannas have large paddle-shaped leaves up to 1m/3ft 3in long that grow to form an upright, loosely cylindrical shape from which the flower spikes emerge in late summer. The flowers themselves are lily-like, usually bright red or orange. Many varieties are available, such as *C. indica* 'Purpurea' with purple-tinged leaves, *C. iridiflora* with huge bluish green banana-like leaves and rose-pink flowers and *C. striata* with variegated foliage. Plant in a fertile soil in full sun.

Clematis tangutica

A vigorous and fast-growing deciduous clematis with a reputation as the best of all the yellow-flowered varieties.

C. tangutica grows to a maximum height of 5m/16ft with densely entangled foliage of sharply toothed green leaflets that will transform a wall, fence, low roof or pergola in sun or partial shade. A crowd of nodding lemon-yellow bell-shaped flowers processes down the stems from late summer well into autumn when they are joined by silk-stranded seedheads. Plant, with the roots shaded, in a rich fertile soil.

Crocosmia 'Lucifer'

In the second half of summer sprays of 'devilish' deep crimson trumpet flowers lean out on wiry stems over the upright, spiky light green leaf blades of this hardy perennial that grows to 1.2m/4ft. The foliage has a grass-like appearance that makes a strong accent in a mixed herbaceous border – especially when planted in random groups – and it glows golden-green when illuminated by the sun. *C.* 'Solfaterre' has bronze leaves with apricot flowers and grows to 60cm/2ft. Plant in well-drained soil in sun.

Dahlia 'Bishop of Llandaff'

There is a whole host of dahlias that will bring late summer colour to your garden and of these, *D.* 'Bishop of Llandaff' is one of the most stylish. This tender tuberous perennial puts up 90cm/3ft stems with an apron of dark, metallic, reddish black pointed ferny foliage. On its own, this leaf colour makes a strong presence among other plants, particularly in an exotic sunny border, and offers an effective backdrop to the glowing, peony-like scarlet

red flowers that open in late summer and draw attention wherever it is planted. Needs a rich, well-drained soil in full sun. Unless the garden is frost-free, lift tubers in winter, dry out and protect indoors until replanting in late spring.

Echinacea purpurea

Coneflowers are very robust-looking beauties that add substance to a late-summer border, whether planted as clumps for structural colour or interspersed with grasses for a wilder, more natural look. Hardy perennials with flowers like mini-sunflowers, they produce a large orange-brown cone-like centre from which spreads a skirt of pinkish purple petals. An atmosphere of natural, unassuming beauty surrounds these flowers. Try *E. purpurea* 'White Swan' for white petals and golden, greenish brown centres. Plant in rich, well-drained soil in sun.

Eupatorium purpureum subsp. maculatum 'Atropurpureum'

A touch of colour for the banks of a stream, pond or pool or the back of a border where the soil is reliably moist. *E. purpureum* subsp. *maculatum* 'Atropurpureum' is a tall-growing form

Tricyrtis formosana

Echinacea purpurea

Hemerocallis

of Joe Pye weed with stiff purple stems and pointed purple-tinged leaves that reaches a stately 2.2m/7ft. From late summer to autumn it carries flat, rosy-purple flowerheads at the top of its stems that make a natural combination with the flowers of tall grasses such as *Calamagrostis* and *Miscanthus* and the large, rounded foliage of marginal plants such as *Darmera* and *Gunnera*. For sun or partial shade; hardy.

Hemerocallis

Daylilies grow well in most soils as long as there is some moisture available. Their crowded clumps of bright green, strap-like leaves – up to 90cm/3ft tall in some varieties - are a structural presence in the developing garden of early spring and their open, often fragrant, lily-like trumpet flowers bring yellows, oranges and reds to the garden from late spring through to late summer. The combination of their lush foliage and bold flowers makes a strong contribution to flower beds and herbaceous borders – and adds substance when randomly placed in a carefree, natural design. *H.* 'Stafford' has glowing red flowers with a yellow throat. All prefer sun.

Kniphofia

An upright, exotic-looking architectural thrill for a bed or border in late summer. Red hot pokers spread a nest of coarsely textured, long, narrow leaf blades that remain all year round (N.B. a favourite hiding place for snails).

From mid- to late summer they puncture the air with their stiff, erect stems topped with bright red, orange and yellow flowerheads that glow luridly, giving all that surrounds them a sense of dowdy modesty. A supreme selection is *K. uvaria* 'Nobilis' which reaches a towering 2.5m/8ft. 'Little Maid' is a shorter-growing form. Plants like this need space, with a deep, fertile soil in full sun.

Rosa rugosa

A tough, robust wild shrub rose with very prickly stems and leathery, bright green wrinkled leaves. Thanks to its tolerance of salt-laden winds, it is useful in coastal gardens and its pollution resistance sees it often used on banks along motorways. It makes a very good hedging plant – growing as high as 2.5m/8ft – but has qualities far beyond mere function. Very fragrant pinkish lilac single cupped flowers open from summer into autumn and are followed by bright red, fat juicy hips. *R. rugosa* 'Alba' has silky white petals. Likes a fertile, well-drained soil in sun.

Sedum 'Herbstfreude'

A clump-forming hardy perennial that starts its year in the spring with fleshy grey-green shoots that develop into succulent leaves and stems through the summer. Fat waxy buds, at the tips of the stems, open into crowded plateaux of tiny green flowers that quickly colour to pink and deepen in late summer to deep bronze, then a rich earth red. These flowerheads still look

good even after the seeds have ripened and their skeleton is all that remains. For a well-drained soil in full sun.

Tricyrtis formosana

Toad lily is a modest, exotic beauty for a sheltered shady spot. It is an upright hardy perennial with 12cm/5in long, deep glossy green leaves, spotted a darker purplish green, on stems that grow to 80cm/2ft 8in. The small 2.5cm/1in wide, lily-like, elaborate star-shaped flowers are pure to pinkish white with yellow throats and reddish mauve spots; they open in late summer. Combine with large-leaved exotics such as ligularias or plant among ferns in a woodland garden. Grow in moist, well-drained soil in shade.

Verbena bonariensis

A hardy perennial of elegance and poise with the self-seeding vigour of a foxglove, *V. bonariensis* is a stunning, slimline late-summer beauty. With stiff, branching, upright dark green stems, it raises clusters of tiny lilac-mauve flowers that hover like exotic insects at intervals up to a height of 2m/6ft 6in. These flowers, appearing from mid- to late summer, work their magic as they infiltrate the flowering spikes of grasses, rise up over clumps of lavender and rosemary and enliven the monochromatic foliage that is all that remains of many perennials after they have flowered in a herbaceous border. Likes a moist, well-drained soil in full sun.

Autumn colour

With the onset of autumn the frenzy accompanying the growth, flowering and productivity of plants slows to an almost teetering halt. A stillness takes over as sap stops rising, fruits and seeds ripen and earthy colours wash through beds and borders.

Acer palmatum 'Osakazuki'
One of the most outstanding ornamental Japanese maples for autumn colour, this is a shrubby deciduous tree that matures to a height of about 6m/20ft with a similar spread. Beautiful deeply cut leaves, 12cm/5in wide with 7 lobes, open in spring to an orange-olive colour that turns bright green in summer. In autumn this tiered, exotic specimen earns its reputation as the leaves take on a vivid brilliant crimson colouring. Best grown under dappled shade in a moist, well-drained soil with protection from cold winds and late frosts.

Aconitum carmichaelii
Monkshood holds back its atmospheric, bowed blue flowers until the heat of summer has passed. An upright-growing perennial with fairly thick, leathery basal leaves that are divided into 3-5 lobes, *A. carmichaelii* sends a flowering spike up to 1.8m/6ft in early autumn. The blue or violet flowers are downward-pointing and look like miniature monk's hoods as they open beside the tall stem. Adds a touch of graceful height to the back of a border or a shady planting of mixed ferns in moist soil; needs staking in windy areas. Fully hardy. (This plant is highly toxic.)

Anemone x hybrida
Japanese anemones are among the most valued autumn-flowering hardy perennials. In late summer a crowd of mid-green basal leaves gives way to

Acer palmatum 'Osakazuki'

slender, branching stems that raise graceful pale pink open-faced flowers – with golden-yellow stamens – up to a height of 1.5m/5ft. These lofty late flowers bring fresh faces to enliven the delicate silhouettes of grasses and other perennials gone to seed and are great for filling gaps in the back of a border. *A. x hybrida* 'Honorine Jobert' has milky white flowers. Vigorous plants that will spread through their suckering stems, Japanese anemones are best placed in moist, fertile soil in sun or partial shade.

Callicarpa bodinieri var. giraldii
The beauty berry is a fairly non-descript deciduous, hardy shrub through the earlier part of the year, with branching stems and grey-green leaves. In the second half of summer things start to look up, with panicles of tiny pinkish lilac flowers that lead to the triumphant stage of this 2m/8ft

tall shrub's embellishment. In autumn clusters of synthetic-looking violet and lilac-purple, bead-like berries appear at intervals along the stems and stay until well after the rose-purple-tinted autumn leaves have fallen. Seems to fruit best when planted in a group, as well as after a hot summer. Needs fertile soil in sun or partial shade.

Ceratostigma willmottianum
A deciduous hardy shrub that makes a loose, spreading mound, 1.4m/5ft wide, that is ideal for the front of a mixed border as a softly structured contrast to tall-growing upright perennials and grasses, even as a low informal hedge up to 1m/3ft 3in. In late summer the mid-green bristly foliage is dotted with a useful addition of many small, star-shaped, forget-me-not blue flowers. When the flowers fade the foliage takes over by turning to a rich, deep reddish bronze. Plant in fertile, well-drained soil in full sun.

Clematis terniflora
A large-growing deciduous clematis that reaches 10m/33ft. The dark green foliage that often has silvery central bands hides a mass of tangled stems from which the current year's growth produces panicles of 2.5cm/1in long, star-shaped, hawthorn-scented white flowers. These flowers – which appear in autumn – extend the flowering season beyond the fading blooms of other climbers such as roses, jasmine and honeysuckle. Plant in rich, well-drained soil against a sunny wall with roots in shade; cut back previous year's growth to two strong buds every spring once established. Needs a hot summer to flower well in temperate climates.

Colchicum autumnale
Meadow saffron is a perennial plant that grows from a corm (solid stem base) to produce large crocus-like flowers of upright petals. These flowers, that appear without leaves, grow straight up out of the ground to form a goblet shape of soft mauve petals to about 10cm/4in tall. Increasing their

Vitis coignetiae

Callicarpa bodinieri **var.** *giraldii*

bark coloration, plant in full sun and cut all stems down to within two buds of the base in early spring.

Cotinus coggygria

The smoke bush is a useful foliage plant that combines well with uniform clipped evergreens such as Portugal laurel, yew and holly, where its rounded soft-green foliage makes a billowing contrast with their more structured form. Light brown panicles of flowers cover the plant in midsummer and fade to a smoky grey, then the leaves blaze with yellow, orange and brilliant red autumn colour. *C. coggygria* 'Royal Purple' has deep purple summer foliage. Frost hardy, grows to 5m/16ft in fertile soil in sun or partial shade.

Euonymus alatus

A twiggy, rounded deciduous shrub that makes a soft, comfortable profile in a mixed shrub border. *E. alatus* grows to a height of 2m/6ft 6in with horizontal fan-like branches that hold out the small 7cm/3in dark green leaves to a width of 3m/10ft. When the leaves fall in winter, they reveal the bark with its characteristic four corky, wing-like outgrowths that run along all stems. But before this the entire shrub glows like a hot coal with bronze, orange and lurid dark red coloration of the leaves. *E. alatus* 'Compactus' is a neat globular dwarf variety that reaches 90cm/3ft. Both are hardy and like well-drained soil in sun or shade.

Liquidambar styraciflua

Sweet gum is a fairly fast-growing hardy deciduous tree for a garden with enough space to accommodate its pyramidal upright shape – eventually 25m/80ft tall with a spread of 12m/40ft. Stately enough to be an individual specimen in a lawn, and delicate enough to include in a woodland planting among ornamental maples and multi-stem birches, *L. styraciflua* bursts into flames at summer's end when its glossy, palmate foliage turns orange, red and glowing purple. Likes a slightly acidic fertile soil in sun or part shade.

Pennisetum orientale

A low, mound-forming deciduous perennial grass with tufts of narrow arching, hairy, dark green leaf blades, 20cm/8in long. From midsummer small, cylindrical bottlebrush-like flower spikes create a wavering silvery pink halo that extends the mounded shape of the foliage to about 45cm/18in. The flowers will fade to a creamy light brown and carry their intricate silhouette through the winter. Warrants planting in a block all on its own in a minimal design and, for a less formal effect, will enhance the impact of other sun-lovers such as architectural bronze fennel, *Echinacea purpurea* and *Achillea* 'Feuerland'. Needs a very well-drained soil.

Rhus typhina

The stag's-horn sumach is a hardy deciduous tree or large shrub that spreads itself through suckering stems – if allowed to, it will form a small copse of upright branches. Young stems have velvety red, hair-covered tips that look like young antlers; these produce palm-like foliage with long, narrow leaflets on stems up to 60cm/2ft long. Swayed by the gentlest of breezes, the light green foliage of *R. typhina* creates dappled shade with exotic shadows in sunshine. In autumn the foliage glows with yellow, orange and red tints before falling. Needs well-drained soil in either full sun or partial shade.

Vitis coignetiae

A triffid among climbers, this bold vigorous hardy vine grows up to 15m/50ft tall with huge, plate-sized, hide-like green leaves on woody stems throughout the summer. The coarsely textured, heart-shaped leaves become flushed with orange, scarlet and deep reddish brown tints at the arrival of autumn. Needs enough space to clamber freely – or there is no point in planting it. The roots should be in rich, well-drained, preferably neutral or alkaline soil with its stems and foliage in sun or partial shade.

numbers in any planted area as time passes, colchicums grow well under trees and around the edges of deciduous shrubs – perfect for autumn colour in a carefree woodland garden. See bulb catalogues for all the *Colchicum* varieties available. Plant in fertile, well-drained soil in sun.

Cornus alba 'Sibirica'

A deciduous hardy dogwood that grows to a maximum height of 3m/10ft, *C. alba* 'Sibirica' has an upright fluted profile of inter-crossing smooth, thin woody stems that are coloured a fiery bright red when still young. As the 10cm/4in dark green leaves colour to reddish orange in the autumn, and the foliage of surrounding plants begins to fall, the lurid bark comes into its own, creating startling, vibrant lines that ignite the muted tones of a shrub border, woodland glade or waterside planting. For best

Climbers

Climbing plants bring a random effect to a garden that livens up the predictable nature of static planting. Some are best left to sprawl and work their magic, others respond well to training and pruning.

Akebia quinata

Known as the chocolate vine, thanks to its deep chocolate-purple flowers that hang in small panicles amid light green rounded leaflets. The flowers of this hardy evergreen climber are an exotic sight in late spring when they open to waft their spicy vanilla fragrance, sometimes producing 10cm/4in long, greyish violet, dangling sausage-like fruits in autumn. *A. quinata* has a sprawling, tangled look as it scuttles over and around walls, trellis, pergolas and dead trees, its leaves comprising 5 or more rounded, oblong light green leaflets. Plant in fertile soil in sun or partial shade.

Clematis armandii 'Snowdrift'

A spring-flowering extravagance, this vigorous evergreen climber pours out cascades of 5cm/2in wide saucer-shaped white flowers that release a rich, heady scent – all the more intense for coming so early in the year. A contorted mass of large, glossy, deeply veined, slightly pointed dark green leaves, 15cm/6in long, covers the twining stems that end up bearing a considerable weight. Make sure any supports or trellis are sturdy and firmly anchored. Needs a sheltered position with well-drained soil in full sun.

Hedera helix

Common ivy is perhaps the hardiest and most resilient evergreen climber available to gardeners. As long as your walls are intact and you can keep this rapid and vigorous grower in check, it is invaluable for enlivening dark corners. I prefer smaller-leaved varieties:

H. helix 'Sagittifolia' with greenish purple stems and 5cm/2in long, arrow-shaped dark green leaves; *H. helix* 'Goldheart' with pink young stems and a golden yellow splash in the centre of each 8cm/3in long, dark green leaf; *H. helix* 'Erecta' with strange, stiffly upright, self-supporting stems to 90cm/3ft. Prefers a fertile soil but will handle most conditions.

Humulus lupulus 'Aureus'

A scampering golden climber ideal for telegraph poles, dead trees, columns and walls. The golden hop drags a mantle of tough, hairy golden yellow-green foliage with it as it scales all obstacles. Vibrant 3-fingered leaves are produced on rapidly growing tangled, fibrous stems, joined in autumn by panicles of cone-shaped fruits used to make beer or as dried flowers. Plant in a fertile, well-drained soil in full sun for best foliage colour. Dies back to ground level in the winter.

Hydrangea anomala subsp. petiolaris

One of the most popular of all climbing plants. On cold, north-facing walls, fences or dead trees – up to 20m/65ft in height – *H. anomola* subsp. *petiolaris* is in its element. Ideally suited to a shady spot, this vigorous, deciduous woody climber will scale the heights unsupported, thanks to the short aerial roots with which it attaches itself along the entirety of its stems. In summer, domed white lacecap flowerheads lean out from the bright green foliage along the length of its stems. Needs fertile, moist, well-drained soil.

Jasminum officinale

From mid- to late summer, common jasmine produces a succession of small white flowers, opening from pink-tinged buds, that release a characteristic strong sweet fragrance. A woody climber, deciduous in all but sheltered regions, it can reach up to 12m/40ft when planted in fertile, well-drained soil in full sun. Often trained along trellis, over arches and mixed with climbing roses and honeysuckle on pergolas, once established, jasmine flowers reliably, and in great profusion. *J. x stephanense* has a more delicate, exotic look but is less hardy.

Lonicera periclymenum

Common honeysuckle is a hardy deciduous woodland climber, native to the British Isles. In the wild, it clambers over hedges, through saplings and into the canopies of older trees while its roots hide in moist, semi-shaded, rich soil. It is a must in cottage gardens for an arbour, arch or over a doorway with deliciously fragrant whorls of scented white, yellow and often red-flushed flowers that open in the second half of summer. There are many cultivated forms, such as *L. periclymenum* 'Belgica', which is ideal for training on supports in containers, growing to no more than 3m/10ft, and *L. periclymenum* 'Serotina' whose dark purple, pink-centred flowers appear from midsummer until the first frosts.

Parthenocissus henryana

A delicate, less rampant form of its familiar relative, Virginia creeper (*P. quinquefolia*), this vigorous, self-clinging deciduous climber grows to 10m/30ft, attaching itself to surfaces with short suction pads. This makes it ideal for camouflaging unattractive masonry, even small buildings, with its wall-hugging foliage. The pointed, 5-fingered deep green leaves – whose veins are picked out in white, pink and later purple – turn a rich bright red in autumn. Likes a well-drained soil and displays better leaf colour when it is grown in shade.

Passiflora caerulea

The passion flower does everything with the zest its name implies. A sprawling evergreen climber, with dark green, 5-fingered glossy leaves, that climbs trees, sheds and anything with which it can entwine its tendrils. The striking flowers are a definite match for all this exuberance and energy with a 10cm/4in star-shaped base of splayed, pink-flushed white petals and a purple, blue and white-banded centre. *P. caerulea* 'Constance Elliot' has fragrant ivory-white flowers. Hardy in milder areas, the passion flower will be cut back to ground level by hard frosts.

Rosa 'Veilchenblau'

A subtle, seductive rose with sweet, fruit-scented, dusky maroon flowers that often show a white flush on some of the petals. Although classed as a rambler, *R.* 'Veilchenblau' grows to a modest 5m/16ft. Its midsummer flowers turn bluish lilac before fading with a greyish tint, holding their colour best when planted in partial shade. Ideal for clambering over an arch or rose bower in a romantic corner, where it will mix well with pinks, like *R.* 'Francis E. Lester', and whites, like *R.* 'Félicité Perpétue'. Needs a fertile, moist, well-drained soil.

Sollya heterophylla

The Australian bluebell creeper is a gentle, twining, evergreen climber that needs a moist, fertile, well-drained soil and a sheltered, sunny or part-shaded site. With protection from frost using horticultural fleece, it will survive winter outdoors in cooler climates. From mid- to late summer hanging clusters of dainty bluebell-like, bright blue flowers open against the glossy dark green leaves to be followed by small blue bean-like fruits.

Trachelospermum jasminoides

Star jasmine wafts its heavy, heady scent through gardens from mid- to late summer. This fragrance, which reaches almost narcotic strengths at dusk after a long hot day, is produced

Humulus lupulus 'Aureus'

Tropaeolum speciosum

Wisteria floribunda 'Alba'

from small star-shaped flowers that unfurl from pointed buds against a backdrop of smart, glossy dark green leaves, 8cm/3in long. Used as sprawling ground cover where climate permits, this medium- to slow-growing evergreen climber has a Mediterranean look when clipped into a neat hedge against

a wall or fence. It needs fertile, well-drained soil in full sun with the protection of a sunny wall in cooler areas.

Tropaeolum speciosum

The so-called flame creeper is a dashing streak of bright scarlet that will warm up the dark, moody tones of, say, a yew or box hedge from midsummer to autumn. This stunning perennial climber, with its spray of red nasturtium-like flowers, prefers to have its roots in shaded, richly composted leafy soil. *T. speciosum* dies back to ground level in winter where its roots will tolerate frosts to about -10°C/14°F. It will grow to a height of 3m/10ft in full sun or partial shade – all it needs is something to climb or clamber over.

Vitis 'Brant'

An ornamental hardy grape vine grown expressly for its abundant foliage. *V.* 'Brant' is a vigorous deciduous climber with broad, 22cm/9in long, deeply lobed bright green leaves that crowd across the new growth, from woody stems, as it scales walls and other obstacles by means of twining tendrils. Achieving a maximum height of 7m/23ft, the leaves turn deep bronze-red in autumn, the veins remaining green to give a marbled effect. These tints are accompanied by large bunches of small, sweet purple grapes. Choose a sunny spot with fertile, well-drained soil.

Wisteria floribunda 'Alba'

This Japanese wisteria has exceptionally long 60cm/2ft racemes of spice-scented, pea-like white flowers that hang down from its bushy, vibrant green foliage. A vigorous deciduous climber for a sunny wall, fence or pergola, where its flowers hang in scented veils. *W. floribunda* 'Alba' can reach 10m/33ft and in time will grow thick, sinuous stems that can be pruned into a framework to produce large flower trusses in early summer and maintain a sculptural presence as a bare structure in winter. Needs moist, well-drained soil in full sun. Hardy, but flowers can be caught by late frosts. Seedpods are poisonous.

Foliage plants

Flowers are not the only rewards of a diverse planting. Foliage brings innumerable variations of colour, tone, texture and pattern to complement these sought-after blooms, their fruits and their seedpods with a suitable backdrop.

Fatsia japonica 'Variegata'

Aralia elata 'Variegata'

A graceful deciduous tree with an open, tiered profile. Layers of horizontal branches break into long compound leaves that create dappled shade for an underplanting of ferns as well as space for the leaves of shrubs like *Hydrangea quercifolia* or *Phyllostachys nigra* to infiltrate and combine well with them. The dark green foliage looks as though it has been accidentally brushed against newly painted walls to give it its random creamy edges. Leaves stretch up to 1.2m/4ft away from the spine-covered woody stems that give it the common name, devil's walking stick. Plant in rich, well-drained soil in sun or partial shade and protect from destructive winds.

Asplenium scolopendrium

The hart's-tongue fern has flat, strap-like, bright green fronds that grow vertically to 45cm/18in. It combines well with delicate herbaceous perennials like *Geranium phaeum*, *Campanula persicifolia* and *Astrantia major* in shady, carefree plantings, as well as beefy sun-lovers such as kniphofias, oriental poppies and peonies. It makes great ground cover and can excite the lower orders of an exotic planting, jostling for position at the feet of gunneras, hydrangeas and phormiums in packed beds. Likes rich well-drained soil.

Athyrium niponicum var. pictum

The Japanese painted fern is a beautiful multi-coloured deciduous perennial

Gunnera manicata

that unobtrusively inhabits moist, rich soil in dappled shade. A plant that you are more likely to notice on the second or third look around a garden, and very rewarding when you do. Delicate, deeply cut, 30cm/12in long silver-green leaves, often with a pink blush across them, are held above the ground on deep red stems. A subtle beauty for a tranquil corner and striking in the atmospheric minimalism of a Zen garden, *A. niponicum* var. *pictum* also makes a decorative ground cover. Protect from heavy frosts with a good mulch in winter.

Catalpa bignonioides 'Aurea'

This golden form of the Indian bean tree is a luxuriant, bright, exotic-looking specimen that is hardy enough for inclusion in the majority of gardens. The 25cm/10in long, heart-shaped leaves are bronze when they first open, then lighten to a bright, sunny

Hosta sieboldiana var. *elegans*

golden-green. In addition to this stunning foliage, white foxglove-like, heavily scented flowers are followed by long, stringy bean pods that stay on the tree till after the leaves have fallen in the autumn. Plant in fertile, well-drained soil in full sun with protection from strong winds. Grows to 10m/33ft.

Euphorbia mellifera

The honey spurge – so called for the rich sweet scent of its spring flowers – is a rounded, evergreen shrub whose distinctive, furred mid-green leaves with glowing golden midribs grow to a length of about 25cm/10in. Definitely on the exotic list, *E. mellifera* combines well with bamboos, fatsias and pittosporums but. to give a more traditional garden a twist. try it alongside *Rosa* 'William Lobb' with an underplanting of campanulas and self-sown *Verbena bonariensis*. Can reach 2.5m/

8ft in perfect conditions – well-drained soil in full sun, protected from frosts.

Fatsia japonica

A very versatile and tough performer that can create dramatic outlines, even in dry shade. *F. japonica* is an evergreen shrub with large, glossy, many-fingered dark green leaves that look like giant claws. Because it is able to handle difficult conditions it is quite commonly used and often unfairly overlooked by those seeking something different. A fatsia will grow to 2.5m/8ft in a reasonably fertile soil and break the monotony of masonry or provide a screen for privacy or camouflage. In late summer, *F. japonica* produces strange flowerheads that resemble clusters of frosted asteroids.

Festuca glauca

A bristling, clump-forming evergreen perennial grass with fine, tufted blue-grey foliage that grows stiffly upright. *F. glauca* looks like a small arrested explosion in a bed when its 30cm/12in profile combines with other plantings. It suits containers – particularly terracotta and lined galvanized steel – and is often used in modern designs as stylish ground cover with a reflective metallic hue. *F. glauca* is fairly drought-tolerant and needs a poor, well-drained soil in full sun.

Foeniculum vulgare

Fennel is a perennial herb with extremely fine, feathery aromatic foliage. Slender, tall hollow stems grow to 1.8m/6ft and spread their airy foliage – allowing neighbouring plants to infiltrate and make beautiful and subtle combinations or striking contrasts. Fennel creates a translucence of billowing bluish grey greenery through which annuals such as nasturtiums, love-in-a-mist and peas can wander in an ornamental vegetable or herb garden. *F. vulgare* 'Purpureum' is a bronze variety often used in herbaceous borders where it sets off the burning reds of crocosmias, dahlias and poppies. Umbels of yellow flowers appear in mid- to late summer and produce the seeds that are used in cooking and herbal medicine. Needs fertile, well-drained soil in full sun.

Gunnera manicata

Giant of giants, this huge herbaceous perennial can conceal secret worlds beneath its 2m/6ft 6in wide, toothed, hide-like leaves that stand on stiff, spiked stems to a height of 2.5m/8ft. The rounded, rough-textured leaves – that can each cover 2.5sq.m/25sq.ft – are deeply furrowed and undulate along broad veins that run from sharply lobed edges towards the centre. A truly prehistoric profile, aptly suited to an exotic planting, as a water plant beside a pond, pool or stream, or as a garden's focal point, *G. manicata* can easily camouflage a garden shed or an uninspiring wall. Likes sun or partial shade, with its roots in very rich, moist soil with a heavy mulch of organic manure. In winter fold dead leaves over the crown; in cold areas mulch thickly with straw as well, to protect the crown.

Hosta sieboldiana var. elegans

A giant hosta (plantain lily) with huge ribbed, fleshy blue-grey leaves that crowd into a dense clump. A perennial crown produces the 30cm/12in long leaves in spring – much to the delight of snails and slugs the world over. Pale lavender flowers follow in midsummer, but serious foliage buffs remove these for fear of diminishing the vigour of the plant. Loves moist, rich soil in partial shade; great for containers where snails find it harder to get at them.

Hydrangea quercifolia

Distinctive deciduous hardy hydrangea with rough, mid-green 20cm/8in leaves that resemble a large oak leaf. The foliage forms a loose mounded shape of up to 1.8m/6ft with a broader spread. Loose, cone-shaped panicles of lacy white flowers open in midsummer and just when you thought the show was over, autumn sees the leaves turning a rich, dark rusty purple. Plant in fertile soil in partial shade.

Musa basjoo

The Japanese banana screams exotica in any garden. Owing to its ability to tolerate reasonably low temperatures, it now makes an appearance in many gardens in parts of the world where its profile would previously have been the stuff of fantasy. As long as you wrap the hard, papery stem with straw or old carpets in winter, you can add to your foliage portfolio the 3m/10ft long, bright green leaf blades that will stretch into view through the summer months. Needs a rich soil in full sun or dappled shade with shelter from damaging winds.

Ophiopogon planiscapus 'Nigrescens'

Among the most striking ground-cover plants available. An evergreen perennial grass with narrow, strap-like, 30cm/12in long leathery leaves that are so dark a purple they look almost black. Though modest in size, the colour of its narrow leaves gives it great potential for dramatic combinations with variegated foliage and a wide variety of flowering plants. Makes a strong candidate for block-planting in minimal and modern designs where it sets off materials like glass, steel and sawn stone in great style. Plant in a rich, moist, well-drained soil in sun or partial shade.

Pleioblastus variegatus

An elegant, low-growing variegated bamboo whose predominantly dark green leaves look as though they have been individually painted along their length with a coarse, uneven brush, to leave creamy white lines of variegation. Combines well with purple flowers and foliage – such as *Knautia macedonica*, *Ligularia dentata* 'Desdemona' and *Ophiopogon planiscapus* 'Nigrescens' – and helps to structure the visual impression of a foliage planting with its bright, clean appearance. Its evergreen foliage and maximum height of 75cm/2ft 6in and spread of 1.2m/4ft makes it a popular ground-cover plant. Needs full sun to promote good variegation and a rich soil.

Ground cover

The leaves and flowers of ground-cover plants can bring tone and texture to lower-level plantings. These living 'carpets' fill in gaps, providing a foil for the foliage and outline of more focal plants.

Ajuga reptans **'Catlin's Giant'**

An invaluable evergreen ground-cover plant that manages to combine an unparalleled performance with exotic delicacy and beauty. Horizontal stems reach out from the plant and continually set root along their length. The 'Speedy Gonzalez' of ground-cover plants, it hugs the soil and keeps low, like an army of ants on the march. *A. reptans* 'Catlin's Giant' has large, shiny bronze-purple leaves about 15cm/6in long and adds to them spikes of deep blue flowers in early summer. It makes a stunning combination with golden hostas and *Milium effusum* 'Aureum' (Bowles' golden grass). Prefers shade – tolerating even full shade – with moist, humus-rich soil.

Alchemilla mollis

A soft-leaved, low-growing herbaceous perennial ground cover that forms clumps of fan-shaped, hairy mid-green leaves to about 45cm/18in. A froth of lime-green flowers floats above the foliage in midsusmmer but the beauty is in the leaves when the tiny hairs catch and hold raindrops like sprays of diamonds. Self-seeds very freely indeed, so dead-head if you want any chance of control. Loves to run about beneath and between taller-growing perennials in herbaceous borders where it will thrive in a rich soil in full sun or partial shade.

Briza media

A drought-tolerant, deciduous hardy perennial grass that grows to a height of 90cm/3ft. The grassy stems are an unspectacular blue-green in colour and about 15cm/6in in length. They make a dense tuft of bristled foliage up to 30cm/12in wide that sends out stiff stems bearing panicles of greenish purple, heart-shaped flower spikes from midsummer through to autumn when they fade to a light brown. These flower spikes tremble at the slightest breeze, which gives *B. media* its common name of quaking grass. Drought-tolerant architectural ground cover that thrives in well-drained soil and full sun.

Cornus canadensis

Creeping dogwood is a luxuriant, refined ground-cover plant that has short stems surrounded by elegant 4-10cm/1½-4in long, mid-green leaves, pointed at their tip and broad at their base. These whorled leaves cushion the opulence of the blooms themselves – holding them almost as proudly as you would yourself – which comprise 2.5cm/1in oval white bracts with tiny green and yellow flowers at their centre that show from spring into summer. Growth is slow but definitely worth waiting for. Plant these creeping perennials 30cm/12in apart in moist, acidic soil in partial shade.

Galium odoratum

A perfect companion to a woodland planting or a selection of small ornamental trees and mixed shrubs, *Galium odoratum* creates a uniform fresh green ground cover to a height of 25cm/10in and an indefinite spread. The deciduous foliage has a soft-textured appearance with star-like whorls of pointed leaves around square stems (highly aromatic when dried). It can be used to define and soften the edges of paths and borders and to enliven areas in deep shade; it produces sweetly scented, dainty star-shaped white flowers in midsummer. Plant in moist, rich soil in sun or shade.

Hebe pinguifolia **'Pagei'**

A sprawling shrub that keeps its head beneath 25cm/10in and spreads to 1.5m/5ft. The foliage is a mass of tiny rounded, fleshy, leathery leaves, blue-grey in colour, that crowds the surface of the soil where the hebe is allowed to flourish. A profuse dusting of small star-shaped flowers covers the plant in midsummer. Plant in full sun in a light, free-draining soil.

Juniperus horizontalis

Evergreen horizontal junipers are spectacular when given space to really spread themselves out – like giant, beached stingrays they lay their glaucous, aromatic needle-like foliage across the soil. Junipers look very good next to clean, sawn stonework and metallic structures and ornament, and will create a strong ground-based presence in a dry garden. *J. horizontalis* 'Blue Chip' has silvery blue leaves and is a ground-hugging variety that keeps within 20cm/8in of the soil's surface. 'Bar Harbour' spreads up to 1.8m/6ft with steel-blue foliage that turns a mauvish purple in autumn. Fairly drought-tolerant once established, junipers favour a well-drained soil in full sun or light, partial shade.

Lamium maculatum **'Beacon Silver'**

Ideal for brightening the monotony of dull spots between plants in partial or deep shade, this spotted deadnettle has an almost metallic sheen thanks to the silver marking that covers the small 5cm/2in leaves, but for a thin, light green outer margin. In the summer short spikes of white flowers appear to complement the fine silver leaves and bring the height to a maximum of 20cm/8in. Plants spread to

Alchemilla mollis

Lamium maculatum 'Beacon Silver'

Ajuga reptans

about 30cm/12in and should be given a moist, well-drained soil. Clip low after flowering to rejuvenate foliage. 'White Nancy' is another good cultivar.

Luzula sylvatica
Greater woodrush is a native of damp woodland and rocky slopes, which makes it suitable for both shady and exposed situations in the garden. An unassuming but beautiful gentle evergreen grass-like hardy perennial that forms tufts and hummocks of fine, shiny, dark green blade-like leaves to a length of 30cm/12in. Its spread can be indefinite unless restrained. In spring, arching stems to 80cm/2ft 8in produce clusters of tiny mid- to dark brown flowers. Ideal in combination with ferns and broad leaves such as hostas and ligularias. Though it prefers shade, will tolerate sun in consistently moist soil.

Lysimachia nummularia 'Aurea'
Golden creeping Jenny is a perfect common name for this bright, busy little plant that hugs the ground as it scuttles about, forming a fleece of coin-shaped leaves. A deciduous creeping perennial that keeps itself to within 5cm/2in of the soil, *L. nummularia* 'Aurea' is so vigorous it will smother other ground-cover plants that get in its way. Best planted beneath trees such as Japanese maples and shrubs like red dogwood (*Cornus sanguinea*) for stunning contrasts. Will pour over the edge of containers and makes a fine marginal plant at the edge of pools

and streams. Likes moist, well-drained soil in sun or partial shade.

Persicaria affinis
An evergreen perennial with 15cm/6in long, dark green, slender pointed leaves forming a dense mat of upright foliage. Long horizontal stems draw leaves away from the plant's centre across the ground, up to a distance of 1.2m/4ft. In midsummer, they send up an array of crowded 8cm/3in flower spikes that open deep rose-pink then slowly fade to a paler hue. *P. affinis* 'Superba' has foliage that turns a rich dark caramel colour in autumn and *P. affinis* 'Donald Lowndes' starts with pale pink flowers that darken with age. Plant in sun or shade in moist soil; tolerates drought.

Potentilla fruticosa
A deciduous shrub with a gentle, soft appearance in the random, almost cloud-like mounds of pointed leaves that cover a brittle-looking mass of woody stems. Single, open-faced 4cm/1½in wide flowers appear practically throughout the growing season from spring to autumn, making it a useful addition to any garden where the soil is not too rich, drains well and the plants can to thrive in full sun. *P. fruticosa* 'Abbotswood' is a low-growing variety (to 60cm/2ft) which spreads to 1.2m/4ft with white flowers and delicately textured dark blue-green leaves. *P. fruticosa* 'Red Ace' grows to similar dimensions and has stunning bright vermillion-red flowers.

Rosmarinus officinalis Prostratus Group
This unusual form of rosemary is useful in a dry garden where the soil bakes in relentless sunshine and frosts are not severe. A fluid mass of slender leathery grey-green leaves clothes the sometimes contorted, brittle woody stems all through the year and gives off a distinct, refreshing aroma. Plant at foot of an Italian 'pencil' cypress (*Cupressus sempervirens* Stricta Group) and standard olive or bay trees in a formal layout, or use it to cover rock-strewn banks and terraces near seating areas in a more relaxed setting. Tubular pale blue flowers grace plants from spring to early summer, sometimes repeated at the end of summer. Fairly drought-resistant, rosemary should be planted in a poor, freely draining soil in full sun.

Vinca minor 'Atropurpurea'
A rich, deep-magenta-flowered form of lesser periwinkle that provides evergreen cover through dense mats of creeping stems lined with 2-5cm/1-2in long, narrow glossy leaves. The subtly beautiful small flowers perfectly complement the dark green lustrous foliage when they appear from early spring to late summer. Vigorous and invasive, *V. minor* 'Atropurpurea' is best used where little else will grow – make sure you are committed to it before planting. Likes a sunny or partially shaded site in dry soil, making it ideal to plant beneath large trees and at the base of hedges.

Architectural plants

In the chaos and exuberance of a planted garden, architectural plants give us pause for thought. They attract our attention and hold our gaze through their bold sculptural outlines, texture or sheer scale.

Agave americana

Acanthus mollis

Bear's breeches has flowers that you will love to look at but won't want to grasp! The dark green leaves of this perennial often make it through the winter and are bold, beautiful and classy with deeply cut symmetry that is often repeated in the designs found on handles of fine silverware and decorative stonework. Flower spikes rise to 1.5m/5ft in late summer with white flowers encased in purple spiny bracts along their length. Loves a rich soil in sun or partial shade.

Agave americana

Looking as though it has been carved from stone, *Agave americana* is a succulent plant that slowly unfurls its opulence with toothed, grey-green leaves - as fat at their base as they are finely sharpened at their tips – rising to 1.8m/6ft before curling away from the centre of the plant. Try *A. americana* 'Variegata' with yellow margins that fade to white for further accent. Happy in containers or planted out in reasonably fertile, sharply draining soil, *A. americana* must be provided with effective protection from frost; alternatively it should be taken indoors in cold weather.

Allium hollandicum

A unique architectural bulb with slender 90cm/3ft stems supporting a densely packed 10cm/4in globe of purple star-shaped flowers. With their uncharacteristic profile and rich colour, alliums complement many other plants from fine-feathered grasses such as *Miscanthus sinensis* to trees such as laburnum, whose curtains of yellow flowers hang down towards allium flowers in early summer. Plant bulbs in fertile, well-drained soil in a sunny position in the autumn.

Angelica archangelica

A hardy biennial that just keeps getting bigger until it dies after flowering. A blank space in a shady corner will quickly assume a sculptural presence as the 2m/6ft 6in tubular-stemmed structure claims available space and produces 25cm/10in umbels of light yellow-green flowers. *A. gigas* grows slightly less tall but adds the exotic touch of dark purple flowers and stems – striking beside the blue-grey blades of *Phormium tenax*. Both favour a rich, moist soil in sun or partial shade.

Betula utilis var. jacquemontii

The sort of tree that always graces architects' drawings and one of the few deciduous trees that look almost better in the winter months. A very slender, graceful, medium-height multi-stem birch whose peeling white bark singles it out for special attention. The clean, sleek stems appear from just above ground level and support a delicate canopy of light, feathery foliage – ideal for underplanting with cyclamen, ferns and hellebores. Grows to 12m/40ft and likes a moist soil in full sun or partial shade.

Cardiocrinum giganteum

A colossus among bulbs. This gigantic lily takes 3–4 years to build up enough energy to send up a 4m/13ft stem, leaving large, glossy, heart-shaped basal leaves far behind. Each stem is crowned with up to 20 richly scented, 20cm/8in long white trumpet flowers that make it well worth the wait. Favours a cool, sheltered site in rich, fertile, free-draining soil. Protect new growth from frosts in early spring, keep moist in dry spells and feed in spring and summer.

Cupressus sempervirens Stricta Group

Unsurpassed Mediterranean elegance goes hand-in-hand with the slender presence of the Italian cypress. This tall conical evergreen conifer can, in time, reach up to 20m/65ft. The tightly held dark greyish green foliage seems almost afraid to stray from its proximity to the central stem and exudes a cleansing aroma on hot days or when it is crushed. Plant in well-drained soil in full sun, protected from cold winds.

Cynara cardunculus

The cardoon is a statuesque, stately perennial with large, deeply toothed, arching silvery furred leaves that curl out to 90cm/3ft from the base of the plant. Several 1.5m/5ft flowering stems rise up to be crowned with large, thistle-like scaly flowerheads whose purple flowers dazzle from early summer into autumn. Needs a rich, fertile, well-drained soil in full sun. In cold areas mulch the roots in winter with a layer of straw.

Allium hollandicum

Dicksonia antarctica

Dicksonia antarctica

A native of Tasmania and eastern Australia, the soft tree fern is all the rage in Europe for its exotic prehistoric appearance. This derives from its thick fibrous stems – anything up to 6m/20ft tall (with approximately 30cm/12in representing about six years' growth) – and the huge evergreen fronds (up to 2m/6ft 6in long) that unfurl from the crown. *D. antarctica* will thrive in fertile soil and cool partial shade provided it is given protection from frosts in winter. When watering, concentrate your efforts on giving the stem a thorough soaking.

Echium pininana

This glorious plant is exotica personified. A mid- to late summer extravagance, its rosettes of silver-green basal leaves cleave the airways with 1.5–4m/5–13ft stems that produce copious rich blue funnelled flowers. It dies after flowering, usually in its second or third year. Well-drained soil in full sun is a must, along with a protective layer of horticultural fleece through the winter months in frost-prone areas.

Eremurus x isabellinus 'Cleopatra'

The slender, beautiful profile of this foxtail lily rises high above many other herbaceous and annual plantings in borders from early to midsummer. Flower-tipped stems soar from a basal cluster of strap-like grey-green leaves to a height of 1.5m/5ft and open to a glowing pale apricot (a delicate enrichment to mixed grasses and stunning among pale electric-blue delphiniums). Plant in rich, well-drained soil in full sun and mulch the crowns in winter.

Pennisetum alopecuroides

A delicate and minor explosion amid other plantings, the evergreen perennial fountain grass produces a 1.5m/5ft tall clump of massed bright green leaves from which emerges an array of bristled purplish green flower spikes, late summer to autumn. Grow in light, well-drained soil in sun and leave dead foliage as protective mulch until spring.

Phormium tenax

Cleaner, more serene lines cannot be found than those of the New Zealand flax, clump-forming evergreen plants with a striking appearance that is both unified and complex. Their uniformity comes with long, regular, bluish green blade-like leaves up to 4m/13ft long that crowd within the plant's fluted form. A delicate play of tones and shadows creates complex, beautiful movement as the blades rotate in the slightest breeze. For moisture-retentive but well-drained soil in full sun; mulch

through winter in colder areas and protect from strong winds.

Phyllostachys nigra

The arching stems of the graceful black bamboo take on a tone of darkest ebony that is revealed, then hidden, as the bright green foliage, sprouting forth from the upper sections, moves lazily to and fro in the slightest breeze. A tall-growing architectural exotic evergreen, *P. nigra* can reach 5m/15ft, which makes it a perfect choice for screening out unattractive buildings or shading the large leaves of, for example, *Gunnera manicata* or *Hydrangea aspera*. It is ideally suited to planting in a moist, rich, well-drained soil in sun or dappled shade.

Pseudopanax ferox

It is the young specimens of this evergreen New Zealand native that attract the most attention. The toothed lancewood is a truly futuristic-looking tree with a touch of the extra-terrestrial about it thanks to its bony, rigid, downward-pointing leaves – edged in greenish bronze 45cm/18in long spine-tipped teeth – that hang directly from the entire length of sinewy, muscular-looking silver-grey stems. Matures into a bushy rounded head of much shorter leaves with a maximum height of 5.5m/18ft. Hardy in milder areas and happy in dappled shade, with shelter from cool drying winds. Plant one among your camellias to raise eyebrows!

Sisyrinchium striatum 'Aunt May'

A strong architectural accent can be achieved in a modest border with the sleek, 45cm/18in tall, cream-margined grey-green blades and buttery popcorn-covered flowering stems of this sun-loving perennial. It looks great with pale dusty blues – *Geranium* 'Johnson's Blue' – fresh lemony greens - *Alchemilla mollis* – and deep purples – *Ophiopogon planiscapus* 'Nigrescens'. If planted in well-drained soil, it will not suffer from winter waterlogging.

Good container plants

Creating a garden in pots allows you to combine plants with different requirements and to assemble them in soil-free zones such as balconies, stairways, roof terraces, paved areas and window sills.

Acer palmatum

Ornamental Japanese maples are graceful hardy deciduous trees and shrubs that can survive for many years in a container. As slow-growing trees they contribute considerable height – up to 2m/6ft 6in of foliage – to a containerized plant collection while requiring comparatively small pots. In an oriental style garden they are often grown in glazed pots that give additional refinement to their gentle tiered shapes and delicate fingered leaves. *A. palmatum* 'Bloodgood' has dark burgundy leaves with bright red autumn colour; *A. palmatum* var. *dissectum* grows to a horizontal mounded form that looks very good close to water. Plant in sun or dappled shade with shelter from winds and late frosts.

Aeonium 'Zwartkop'

A striking succulent with rosettes of shiny, near-black, dark purple leaves. *A.* 'Zwartkop' makes an interesting inclusion in a group of potted plants in partial shade, where its colour is a stark contrast to the tones of metal, stone or terracotta containers. It extends its short stems of shadow-like foliage into a collection of almost skeletal, metallic-looking heads that set off euphorbias such as *E. characias* subsp. *wulfenii* and *E. mellifera*, as well as phormiums and various grey-leaved architectural plants. Needs the protection of a greenhouse or conservatory in winter. Plant in cactus compost.

Agapanthus Headbourne hybrids

The hardiest of the African blue lilies, *A.* Headbourne hybrids are perennials of architectural grace and beauty. They form a dense clump of fleshy roots that produce a mass of strap-like green leaves to 45cm/18in. For this reason they are often used as ground cover and for retaining soil on sunny banks. From mid- to late summer large globe-shaped open clusters of light to deep blue flowers emerge on 90cm/3ft stems. Agapanthus are said to flower better when the roots become restricted, so plant close together in pots to speed this process. They like a rich, fertile soil in full sun.

Bidens ferulifolia

Planted as an annual in window boxes and pots, often at the feet of lavender, box or other structural plants that lack a low-spreading habit. Bidens soon sprawls in all directions to create a mist of filamentous green foliage, against which literally hundreds of small, golden-yellow daisy flowers shine brightly. The flowers open over a long period from early summer into autumn. Needs a fertile planting compost in full sun and grows up to about 30cm/12in.

Buxus sempervirens

The ultimate topiary plant, box is an extremely slow-growing hardy evergreen shrub with small, rounded dark green leaves. Often used to create the low-hedged structure of parterres and knot gardens, it responds well to clipping, producing dense, firm planes of foliage. Box is clipped into all manner of shapes and looks good in pots among herbs and perennials. As a container subject, such as a curving spiral or a cone shape, it has an architectural profile that sees it used to mark repetition or symmetry in formal designs. Plant in a loam-based compost in sun or partial shade.

Cordyline australis

Bring architecture on to a terrace, patio, pathway – even a broad window sill – with *C. australis*. A handsome spiky-leaved palm-like tree (when it matures) with slender, narrow, blade-like light green leaves that arch away from a central stem. Young plants are virtually stemless and look like elegant fountains of foliage. Older specimens are essential in exotic gardens where, on tall stems, they raise a loose linear canopy above broad-leaved plantings, across which their long, narrow leaves cast spidery shadows. *C. australis* Purpurea Group has dark purple blades. Hardy in milder areas, it can grow to 6m/20ft. Plant in a free-draining loam-based compost.

Erigeron karvinskianus

A busy, freely self-seeding perennial that, once planted, will surprise you year after year as it crops up in new and different locations around your garden. *E. karvinskianus* forms a floriferous carpet of tiny daisy flowers with yellow centres and petals that are pink on opening then turn quickly to brilliant white. A sprawling mass will soon develop and spill out from hanging baskets, window boxes and pots; also ideal in gaps between slabs on a terrace or holes in a wall in a carefree or recycled design. Plant in free-draining loam-based compost in full sun.

Euphorbia characias subsp. wulfenii

An evergreen perennial with small greyish green leaves that sprout horizontally from tall purplish stems. Together they make architectural upright columns of foliage, adding structure to borders and combining well with sun-loving shrubs and perennials. Large, cylindrical, alien-looking lemon-yellow flowerheads

Agapanthus **Headbourne hybrids**

Zantedeschia aethiopica **'Crowborough'**

Tulipa **'Black Parrot'**

Gaillardia x grandiflora

Amazingly hard-working hardy perennials for pots in a sunny position, gaillardias have cheery, open-faced flowers with a cone-like centre and surrounding petals that are mostly red with a lurid yellow halo at their tips. A must for a colourful corner, a window sill or an exotic collection – where there is no fear of exuberance – gaillardias will brighten your days, providing a continuing stream of flowers from mid- to late summer. *G.* x *grandiflora* 'Kobold' grows to 30cm/12in. Plant in a well-drained, loam-based compost and dead-head to keep them blooming.

Lavandula

Pots of lavender are used to line paths, flank doorways, decorate terraces and bring scent to window sills. They can be placed in borders to give height and structure and brought into a potager to attract pollinating insects. Lavender is a perfect container plant: its evergreen silver-grey foliage makes structural mounds and complements terracotta, wafting a sweet fragrance whenever it is brushed against; the flowers add hazy blue height on their slender stems in late summer. Happy in free-draining, fertile to poor soil and full sun, it generally looks after itself. *L. angustifolia* 'Hidcote' is a compact form – good for low hedges.

Strelitzia reginae

If you have the benefit of a conservatory or greenhouse to protect one of these extravagant evergreen perennials through winter in cold areas, then you can join the ranks of tropical gardeners. By planting a bird of paradise in a pot you will be able to enjoy its exotic foliage outdoors in the summer and return it indoors during colder months to watch it flower. The long, smooth, paddle-shaped light green leaves make an upright clump to 1.2m/4ft and in winter and spring the bird-like orange and blue flowers open on stems 1.8m/6ft tall. Plant in a container filled with loam-based compost and place in sun or partial shade.

Trachycarpus fortunei

The Chusan palm is a striking slow-growing evergreen architectural tree with an exotic profile. Frost-hardy, pollution-tolerant and happy in most soils as long as they drain well, all you need do is find it a spot in sun or dappled shade with protection from strong winds. A tapering single trunk produces large fans up to 90cm/3ft across of narrow, shiny dark green leaves on stiff stems that create beautiful long-fingered shadows and clatter together in a breeze. Thanks to its slow growth rate it is happy in a pot filled with fertile loam-based compost.

Tulipa

Tulips are an invaluable source of colour in the developing garden in early to late spring. Planted out in beds, their graceful flowers stand on stiff, upright stems and blaze their colours in a sea of unfolding green. Planted in pots they can be brought close to a window or doorway or placed in gaps in a border and removed after flowering. A multitude of shapes, colours and sizes are available. *T.* 'Black Parrot' has almost black, feather-like petals, *T.* 'Pink Diamond' is pure fluted pink elegance and *T.* 'Bellona' has rounded, golden-yellow, deliciously scented flowers. Plant in manure-enriched loam-based compost and place in full sun.

Zantedeschia aethiopica 'Crowborough'

A luxurious sight at the margins of a water feature in milder areas with its roots in moist, boggy ground, this arum lily is also suited to being container-grown outdoors or in a conservatory. Its large, fleshy leaves, shaped like bright green arrowheads, extend the palette of green tones and outlines in both water gardens and exotic plantings. From midsummer, lavish white, broadly funnelled flowers open on stems up to 1m/3ft 3in tall, each lasting for weeks. Outdoors apply a thick mulch to protect roots in winter when foliage will be cut back by frosts. In containers use manure-enriched loam-based compost.

open from mid- to late spring and add dramatic beauty to the foliage. Grows to up to 1.5m/5ft and is hardy in mild areas. Plant in a sharply drained loam-based compost in full sun – the leaf tones go well with terracotta. Note: for some, the milky white sap is said to be an irritant.

Food plants

Food plants combine edible and decorative potential. In addition to their flowers and foliage, they offer fruits, roots, tubers, bulbs and pods full of flavour to tempt some of our other senses.

Allium schoenoprasum (chives)

A hardy herb that bunches its hollow leaves together like an upright grass, chives are grown for their tapering cylindrical, 60cm/2ft tall, dark green leaves that have a mild, sweet oniony taste. If allowed to, they will produce pale purple flowers from early summer – these are an interesting architectural trinket in a mixed planting of other herbs, but will lessen the flavour of the leaves. Chives can be divided in spring or autumn when they can be potted up and taken indoors to continue growing through winter. Use flowers to decorate salads. Plant in rich, well-drained soil in sun.

Beta vulgaris **Beetroot Group (beetroot)**

Round, tapered, globe-shaped, flat-tened, long or oval – you can choose the shape of beetroot you grow. Dark purple-red, white banded with red and white rings, or yellow – choose the colour too. Beetroot have chard-like crinkled leaves with red or golden-green stems and veins that are tasty in salads or can be cooked like spinach; they also look good in a flower border. The root fattens from mid- to late summer and should be harvested after reaching golf-ball size to be grated, baked or pickled. Moisture levels must be regularly maintained to prevent hardening or splitting of the roots.

Beta vulgaris **Cicla Group (Swiss chard)**

A large-leaved beet whose tough-looking, deeply wrinkled bright green leaves grow on broad stems straight from the ground. Swiss chard is a biennial plant usually treated as an annual for the fresh, chewable leaves that grow in the first year. As an ornamental foliage plant it makes a strik-ing sight in a flower bed, especially the red-stemmed 'Ruby Chard' or yellow, orange and red 'Rainbow Chard' which introduce bold contrast to late-summer perennials like *Echinacea purpurea* and *Agastache foeniculum*. Try letting some overwinter for the extraordinary 8cm/3in wide, coloured stems up to 1.2m/4ft in the second year. Likes rich, free-draining soil in sun or part shade.

Cucurbita maxima (pumpkins and squashes)

Very vigorous annuals that produce a sprawling mass of hairy, brittle stems and rough, rounded, dark green leaves. Some trailing varieties can actually be trained as climbers – an extraordinary sight when grown over an arch that becomes festooned with their heavy pendulous fruits. From the pumpkin 'Atlantic Giant', at up to 317kg/700lb more a piece of furniture than a piece of fruit (definitely not for training), to blue-skinned 'Queensland Blue' and the decorative green- and cream-striped orange 'Turk's Turban' squash-es, these are a striking attraction. Can be grown in large containers in rich, moisture-retentive compost in sun.

Cydonia oblonga (quince)

A small, hardy deciduous tree with a spreading canopy of dark green leaves that in late spring bears delicate mag-nolia-like, pale pink open-faced flow-ers which give it an air of opulence. Through summer, small furred fruits swell to branch-breaking weights and end up looking like large yellow pears. Quinces are hard fruits with a rich, exotic perfume that are best baked. Planted in fertile, well-drained soil in full sun, *C. oblonga* will grow to 5m/16ft with a similar spread.

Cynara scolymus (globe artichoke)

Edible distant cousin of the cardoon, this is an architectural stunner for a potager or a flower border where it will require space to grow to its regal stature of 1.8m/6ft with a spread of up to 1.2m/4ft. Large, deeply lobed, hairy silver basal leaves arch out from the centre where flower spikes are elevat-ed to noble heights. In midsummer, large thistle-like flowerheads – edible in bud form – begin to open with a crown of powdery bluish lilac. They are as delicious to eat as they are to look at. Plant in rich, well-drained soil in baking sun with shelter from winds.

Eruca vesicaria (rocket)

A fast-germinating hot, spicy salad leaf that is ready for picking 7 weeks after sowing. Rocket is a good catch crop to sow between slower-growing vegetables such as cabbages and sprouting broccoli. Can be grown as an individual plant or as a row of cut-and-come-again seedlings, it is also good for planting in containers. Needs a rich, moisture-retentive soil in partial shade to avoid a sun-distilled bitter taste. I let a few plants bolt to produce their pretty 4-petalled white flowers.

Ficus carica (fig)

A medium-sized spreading deciduous tree with large, round-fingered, rough dark green leaves that create deep shade and tropical shadows beneath it. Can be trained against a sunny wall, with its silver-grey stems encouraged into interesting patterns that have sculptural outlines when bare in win-ter. The fruits ripen to green, purple or brown depending on variety – 'Brown Turkey' is the hardiest, with greenish brown fruits. For a good crop of fruit plant your fig in a large container or in the ground with its roots restricted. Needs a sunny spot in rich, well-drained soil.

Lycopersicon esculentum (tomato)

Given a sheltered, sunny position and a fertile, well-drained soil, tomatoes will produce large numbers of delicious fruit on plants from 30cm/12in to 1.8m/6ft tall. Fruits can range from huge meaty monsters weighing up to 0.4kg/1lb each ('Brandy Wine') to tiny cherry-like 2.5cm/1in globes ('Gardener's Delight'), with colours from yellow, orange to red as well as striped varieties ('Tigerella'). Plant out seedlings after all risk of frosts is over and feed with tomato fertilizer once the first trusses form. Many smaller varieties are ideal in pots and hanging baskets.

Ficus carica (fig)

Allium schoenoprasum (chives)

Morus nigra (mulberry)

A mulberry tree is an extravagant and decadent luxury that in many gardens becomes a focal point as it matures to a thick, wrinkled trunk with a heavy canopy of heart-shaped leaves. In summer the dark green, hairy foliage becomes home to an intoxicated rabble of teetering pigeons and songbirds gorged on juicy fruits that crowd the branches. *M. nigra* – the hardy black mulberry – will turn any paving beneath it purple with fallen fruits. Mature trees usually collapse with age, continuing to grow and fruit in a reclining position for years afterwards – bear this in mind when you choose a site. Plant in fertile soil in full sun and put away your white clothes. Grows to 12m/40ft with a slightly wider spread.

Phaseolus coccineus (runner beans)

An annual climber that grows so fast you can almost watch as its twining stems snake their way up supporting hazel or bamboo bean rods. Often planted for purely ornamental purposes – over arbours and arches and up fences, trellis or large shrubs – runner beans produce clusters of white or scarlet flowers along their stems. The slightly shiny, rough, delicious green pods that hang down after the petals have fallen can be up to 50cm/20in. Plants grow up to 3m/10ft and need sturdy support. Grow in a deep, fertile, moisture-retentive soil in full sun.

Lycopersicon esculentum (tomato)

Pisum sativum (peas)

From among a tangle of supportive dead willow cuttings comes a harvest that, for many, will trigger memories of their first tastes in the garden as children. Protruding from grey-green rounded leaves on sinewy stems that clasp at the supporting willow with tendrils and clamber toward the sun, white hanging flowers develop flattened pods which fatten as their sweet contents swell, to produce a taste to take you back in time – and all in just 12 weeks. Height up to 60cm/2ft. Where space permits, sow fortnightly in succession in fertile soil in a protected, sunny site and provide support.

Rheum x hybridum (rhubarb)

A hardy perennial with large, rounded dark green leaves – up to 1m/3ft 3in across – that are held on stiff, upright bright red stems. These stems are harvested from late winter (if forced beneath a large pot) all the way through to midsummer – they are generally taken a few at a time to prevent weakening the plant. To ensure continued cropping of good stems, do not allow a rhubarb plant to flower. Can be grown in containers, even bin liners, and likes a well-composted soil to feed its hungry, deep fleshy roots. Plant in a sunny position. Note: the leaves themselves are toxic.

Zea mays (sweetcorn)

Looking like a large-leaved bamboo, this robust, tall-growing annual grass reaches 1.5m/5ft with a spread of up to 75cm/2ft 6in. At the top of its tough stem a decorative spray-like panicle of male flowers is produced to fertilize female flowers further down the plant. This architectural-looking flower, along with the 90cm/3ft long dark green wavy leaves, makes sweetcorn worth experimenting with as an annual among grasses and large-leaved flowering perennials in a sunny, sheltered bed with fertile, well-drained soil. And then of course in late summer there are the cobs of golden corn . . . . Can be grown in large tubs or containers.

Aromatic plants

The foliage and flowers of certain plants contain strong infusions of aromatic essential oils to attract beneficial insects. Put your scented plants where you can best enjoy them, for a garden full of fragrance.

Aloysia triphylla

An exhilarating, light refreshing lemon fragrance greets the slightest touch of the foliage on this deciduous tender shrub. Lemon verbena has a modest appearance that is totally eclipsed by its powerful aroma. Its long, slender, coarsely textured light green leaves are dried and made into an infusion, using just a couple of leaves in a cup of boiling water. Where frosts are not a threat, plant in poor, free-draining soil – or grow in a container so that it can be taken indoors in wet and cold spells. Can reach up to 3m/10ft.

Chamaemelum nobile

Chamomile is a vigorous, mat-forming perennial herb that has bright green, almost frayed-looking feathery foliage and a profusion of yellow and white daisies. These flowers, which appear in midsummer, are dried and used to make a tea and the foliage gives off a strong aroma of apples when crushed. *C. nobile* 'Treneague' is a non-flowering, low-growing variety often used for chamomile seats and lawns. Plant in well-drained light soil and full sun.

Chimonanthus praecox

The delicious fragrance of wintersweet is all the more intoxicating as it comes at a time of year when much of the rest of the garden is in sensory denial. Waxy, lemon-yellow bell-shaped flowers open before the leaves on bare branches and lace the late-winter air with perfume. After flowering, *C. praecox* loses most of its appeal, so bear this in mind when planting: place it where neighbouring shrubs and peren-

nials will take on the job of pleasing the eye and olfactory system as the season progresses. Good for training on a sunny wall, it is fully hardy, but late growth may be damaged by autumn frosts. Plant in well-drained soil in full sun. Grows to 2.5m/8ft.

Citrus x meyeri 'Meyer'

The flowers of Meyer's lemon tree are as sweet as the fruit can be bitter – sometimes even more so. Normally grown in containers, so that they can be moved to the protection of a greenhouse or conservatory in cold spells, lemons are commonly clipped into half-standards or fan-trained shapes against walls which gives them an exotic profile on a terrace. Meyer's lemon is a popular compact variety whose rounded fruits follow the deliciously fragrant white flowers that open from mauve-tinged buds from mid-spring to midsummer. Only plant in the ground where temperatures do not drop below 0°C/32°F. Needs moist, free-draining soil in sun.

Cytisus battandieri

Pineapple broom is a spindly semi-evergreen plant that makes a good shrub for a sunny wall where its silver-grey leaves can soak up the warmth and produce a host of bright yellow flowers in 15cm/6in upright racemes. The collective shape of the flowers has the look of small inverted pineapples and gives off wafts of this exotic fruit's fragrance as they appear in midsummer. Only slightly hardy, *C. battandieri* grows to 5m/16ft and needs a fertile, well-drained soil in full sun.

Eucalyptus pauciflora subsp. niphophila

A svelte and distinctive profile accompanies this beautiful, hardy snow gum that, compared with other eucalypts, is fairly slow to mature. As it grows, its grey-white outer bark sheds to reveal strips and blotches of bronze and pale olive, giving it an almost sculptural appearance. When crushed, the bluish, grey-green, flat leathery leaves emit the characteristic aroma that has kept many a cold at bay. Grows to 6m/20ft; needs fertile soil in full sun.

Laurus nobilis

Bay trees are an essential part of a herb or kitchen garden, for the flavouring of their leaves, and also of a Mediterranean garden for the stylish clipped shapes they are often trained to assume. A highly aromatic, slightly menthol odour is released when the evergreen leaves are crushed or cut, making pruning and shaping all the more pleasurable. Bays are frost-hardy and grow relatively fast. They respond well to clipping and shaping, making good hedges, though the clipped forms are often container-grown. Plant in well-drained soil in sun or partial shade.

Lavandula stoechas subsp. pedunculata

French lavender has striking, architectural deep purple flowerheads, crowned with slender, lilac, butterfly wing-like bracts, held above a compact body of thin silver-green leaves on brittle woody stems. In the heat of a long, sunny day the essential oils in the foliage distil an intense resin-like odour of sweet frankincense that will dose any hand or clothing that brushes against it. Plant it where it can be appreciated; a good subject for containers. It grows to 60cm/2ft and is reasonably hardy. Needs a poor, well-drained soil and sunshine.

Lilium regale

A hardy lily that easily warrants a regal title thanks to its tall, arching maroon-flushed stems with short, narrow, grey-green leaves rising up from bulbs to an unfeasible 1.8m/6ft, teetering beneath the sheer numbers of flowers at their tip. These large, 15cm/6in long, white trumpet-shaped blooms have a purple hue on their outer side, with a creamy yellow centre and stamens coated in orange pollen. Added to their stature and beauty is their strong honeysuckle scent that will stop you in your tracks. Plant in containers or beds in rich, free-draining soil in autumn. Likes its roots in shade and its head in full sun.

Magnolia grandiflora

A stately and magnificent slow-growing, semi-hardy evergreen tree or wall shrub that brings a hint of luxury to any garden. It is often chosen as a feature plant, perhaps as a clipped shape such as a cone or half-standard. An impressive coat of 20cm/8in long broad, glossy dark green leaves with a brown felty underside give this plant its presence, but the flowers are beyond all expectation. From mid- to late summer, huge coffee-cup-shaped white flowers, 25cm/10in across, cling to supportive clusters of leaves and exude an intoxicating, sweet lemon scent. Grows well in containers, especially when clipped and kept to a controlled shape; if unrestrained will grow 5–20m/16–70ft in rich, well-drained soil in sun.

Melissa officinalis

Lemon balm has a clear, fresh citrus aroma that can cure a headache with a few sniffs. I often grab a leaf and clasp it to my nose while strolling around on a therapeutic end-of-the-day weeding session. The scent of this perennial herb is released when the hairy, nettle-like 7cm/3in bright green leaves are crushed. Though its visible presence does not outweigh its aroma, it is a useful plant for dry shade. Happiest in a well-drained poor soil in full sun, it will grow up to 1.2m/4ft. *M. officinalis* 'All Gold' has golden-yellow leaves. Cut back before flowering for strong foliage.

Philadelphus coronarius 'Aureus'

A golden-leaved form of mock orange, covered in sweet honey-scented white flowers in midsummer. The bright yellow-gold foliage gives *P. coronarius* 'Aureus' a visual impact that matches the addictive fragrance of its flowers. Combines well with purple acers, *Cotinus coggygria* 'Royal Purple', variegated grasses and dwarf bamboos in exotic plantings, as well as blowsy pink roses and herbaceous perennials in cottage gardens. Plant in well-drained soil in light, dappled shade to prevent foliage from scorching in hot sun and protect from late frosts with horticultural fleece. Grows to 2.5m/8ft.

Pittosporum tobira

Japanese mock orange is a relatively hardy large shrub, resembling Mexican orange blossom (*Choisya ternata*), with thick, leathery, dark green leaves on sturdy stems. It has a tropical, slightly prehistoric look that makes the sophistication of its pungent, heavenly orange scent – that hangs in the air when the clusters of creamy white flowers open from spring to midsummer – all the more surprising and pleasurable. Happy in pots and often used as a hedge in coastal areas owing to its salt-tolerant leaves. Plant in sun or dappled shade.

Rosa 'Cardinal de Richelieu'

A Gallica rose whose rich, deep velvet fully double blooms bring extravagance and opulence to a planting

scheme. The compact, almost globe-like magenta-purple flowers release an intense, slightly spicy-sweet scent when they open in early summer. Plant a hedge of this rose to make a fragrant boundary in a romantic scented garden. Grows to 1.2m/4ft and will tolerate a poor soil but needs a fairly open position in sunshine.

Thymus serpyllum

Evergreen creeping thyme forms low mats of tiny, dark green, pointed oval leaves to 25cm/10in high. A froth of minuscule mauve flowers decorates the foliage, bringing delight to bees in summer. A stubborn, vigorous herb that tolerates being walked upon, it rewards such abuse with wafts of a pungent, almost medicinal, pine aroma. This makes it ideal to plant as ground cover or between stone slabs in a dry garden.

Lavandula stoechas

Magnolia grandiflora

Lilium regale

Water plants

Plants occupy three zones within a body of water.
There are plants that grow at its margins in moist
soil, those that float on pads across its surface and
plants that live within and oxygenate the water.

Acorus calamus 'Variegatus'
Variegated sweet flag is a spreading, graceful hardy perennial that forms dense clumps in the shallow margins of a pond or slow stream. In spring it sends slender, bright green iris-like leaf blades with rich cream and white stripes along their length to a height of 1m/3ft 3in; these are followed in early summer by small 7cm/3in long, horn-like flowers that poke out from the side of central stems. When bruised or crushed, all parts of this plant exude a sweet aroma.

Caltha palustris
Marsh marigold is a hardy marginal aquatic perennial with kidney-shaped, dark green leaves up to 10cm/4in long that are raised a short distance above mud or water. In spring, clumps of bright yellow open-faced flowers resembling large buttercups are produced on 30cm/12in tubular stems. Unrestrained, it scuttles along in rich boggy ground in full sun or it can be planted out in aquatic baskets in shallow water.

Cyperus involucratus
A sedge that produces delicate upward-pointing leaves – looking rather like bare umbrella spokes – on top of 90cm/3ft stiff narrow stems. In summer, rays ending in tiny clusters of yellow flowers spread out from the centre of the leaves to give them a lacy head-dress. More often grown as a house plant, it will happily live in the shallows with its roots submerged, where its delicately architectural, precise profile will contrast well with lax grasses at the water's edge. Foliage will be cut back by frosts in winter.

Darmera peltata
The umbrella plant is so called because of its impressive glossy, dark green, rounded leaves that follow on from strange naked flowering stems. In spring these rise from the ground with flattened heads of pale pink flowers. The coarse, toothed, deeply veined leaves are gunnera-like but much hardier; they grow to a height of 1.8m/6ft and are up to 60cm/2ft across. A bold, architectural marginal plant that needs its roots in a rich, moist soil in a sunny or partially shaded location. The leaves turn to rich reds, purples, oranges and browns in the autumn.

Iris laevigata
A broad-leaved iris which forms loose clumps of pointed, light green foliage in moist, rich soil or shallow water. From among the 80cm/2ft 8in leaves in midsummer, clear mid-blue flowers open their ornate, spreading petals – about 10cm/4in across – in contrast to the regimented blades. *I. laevigata* 'Variegata' is said to be the best white-variegated iris available as it carries interest well beyond the flowering period. Likes a sunny position and is frost-hardy.

Iris pseudacorus
The yellow flag iris is a beautiful hardy perennial that thrives with its roots in fertile, permanently moist soil at the water's edge. Its sleek, light green leaves rocket from mud or water-level in spring to a height of 1.5m/5ft and shimmer in the slightest breeze like upright ripples to match those on the water's surface. In midsummer fattened stems produce bright yellow flowers that look rather like tiny lazy herons flapping through the foliage. *I. pseudacorus* 'Variegata' has bright yellow lines on the young blades that fade to a subtle stripe in summer.

Juncus effusus
A tough, robust evergreen spiky rush with stiff, slender, cylindrical pointed leaves that looks like a splash frozen in motion at the water's edge. A strong presence beside looser grasses and broad-leaved marginals and useful for creating structure and movement in and around water. *J. effusus* fires up its many leafless dark green stems to 45cm/18in and grows in water up to 8cm/3in deep or boggy ground at the water's edge. *J. effusus* f. *spiralis* makes an odd-looking contorted shape with its corkscrew stems, more like an implosion than an explosion. Both are hardy and like sun or partial shade.

Lagarosiphon major
A semi-evergreen, hardy oxygenating plant that grows within slow-moving and still water. *L. major* forms a dense mass of 1m/3ft 3in branching stems that are covered along their length with slender, inward-curling, 2.5cm/1in leaves. Looking like long, green, serpentine pine cones, these crowded stems release valuable oxygen into the water and help to clean up newly established ponds. For best results plant 5–6 branches in aquatic compost and sink in a basket in water up to 1.2m/4ft deep.

Ludwigia grandiflora
A dainty-looking floating marginal and aquatic hardy perennial that traces leafy stepping stones – about the width of a duck's stride – across the water's surface as it sprouts clumps of tiny, rounded leaves along snaking woody stems. In late summer it bears small, bright yellow flowers

the same colour as its relative, evening primrose. You may need to interfere from time to time to keep its invasive tendencies in check. Plant in sun or partial shade in moist, fertile soil at the water's margin or in a basket of heavy loam.

Lysichiton americanus

Yellow skunk cabbage is a dominating, large-growing hardy perennial that will unequivocally make its claim over rich soil at the margin of a pool or pond. It is a favourite marginal plant – where there is space enough for it to be worthwhile – for the crowds of 15cm/ 6in upright flowers that look like a fleet of tiny dinghies stood on end. These bright lemon-yellow flowers appear in spring and are closely followed by broad, glossy green leaves that flap out to a length of 1.2m/4ft and last throughout the summer. *L. camtschatcensis* is slightly smaller with white flowers. Both are frost-hardy and like full sun or partial shade.

Miscanthus sinensis 'Variegatus'

An elegant, soaring, clump-forming hardy perennial grass that will reach up to 1.8m/6ft. Tall, upright, arching stems bear narrow, bluish green leaves striped with white variegation along their length. After a hot summer, panicles of pinkish spikelets are produced in early autumn but this plant is chosen for its foliage. A striking specimen for the water's edge, it casts graceful, intricate reflections over the water beneath.

Nuphar lutea

A robust leathery-leaved yellow pond lily that is hardier and more vigorous than its relative *Nymphaea* (waterlily) and can tolerate moving water. Only for a larger pond, this aquatic perennial with 40cm/16in heart-shaped, bright green floating leaves will soon spread to create shaded water for pond life. Less decorative than waterlilies but perhaps more natural-looking, it holds tight, rounded yellow flowers on short stalks above the leaves in summer. Plant in water up to 1.8m/6ft deep in full sun.

Nymphaea

There are a great number of hardy cold-water waterlilies with flowers from white, yellow and pale pink to deep red, and with growing depths from 10cm/4in to 1.8m/6ft – the deeper the growing depth, the more vigorous the variety. Waterlilies create important shade for pond life in the water below and reduce the potential for blanketweed; it is recommended that no more than 25 per cent of your water's surface should be covered with waterlily leaves. The exotic star-like flowers open on the water's surface during the day and close up at night. *N. alba* is a British native that can handle water up to 1.8m/6ft deep and will spread its rounded, dark green leaves with reddish purple undersides to a floating mat up to 1.8m/6ft across, on which the 20cm/8in white flowers

open in midsummer. To restrict growth, plant in a basket filled with aquatic compost and place in shallower water.

Orontium aquaticum

This hardy aquatic perennial is given the common name golden club after its yellow-tipped flowers that appear in spring. It has submerged and floating 25cm/10in long, light grey-green, broad pointed leaves with a purplish underside. Snaking club-like flower stems are raised just above this foliage and make an unusual-looking clump as their numbers increase. The strange flowers comprise a simple spadix (spike covered with tiny stalkless flowers) with no petals. Plant in the ground in moist boggy conditions at the water's edge or place in aquatic baskets in shallow water up to 45cm/18in.

Phragmites australis 'Variegatus'

The variegated form of a common reed that can be found growing native in Britain. Less invasive than straight *P. australis*, it still has a considerable appetite for unoccupied moist soil in shallow water or at its edge. The sharply tapering 60cm/2ft long, grey-green grassy leaves are lined, when young, with golden-yellow variegation that then fades to white. In late summer its flowering stems, that take it to 3m/10ft, are topped with brownish purple spikelets. Best grown in the safe confines of a submerged container. Hardy and likes full sun.

Nymphaea

Iris pseudacorus

Orontium aquaticum

Drought-tolerant plants

In certain locations long, hot, dry summers are a reliable certainty, often accompanied by thin, sharply draining soil. Rather than battle with such situations, try to use plants that are geared to arid conditions.

Achillea

Hardy, deciduous perennials, many of which produce umbrella-like plates of tiny flowers in colours from pale and bright yellow, through pinks and reds to purple. Like brightly coloured flying saucers these flowerheads, planted amid grasses and perennials, contribute hovering horizontal splashes of colour. Many varieties are available, from low-growing *A. tomentosa* with woolly, fern-like foliage and yellow flowers up to 15cm/6in in height, to *A. filipendulina*, with similar coloration, reaching 1.2m/4ft. The flowers of *A. 'Feuerland'* open terracotta red before fading to sandy, amber tones with age. Flowerheads are often left on into winter for an exquisite dusting of frost.

Agastache foeniculum

A native plant of North America where it grows wild in dry scrub and grassland, *A. foeniculum* (anise hyssop) is a delicate-looking, aromatic, hardy perennial whose association with grasses in the wild can well be repeated in the garden. Planted among *Miscanthus sinensis* 'Gracillimus', *Pennisetum alopecuroides* and *Bouteloua gracilis*, its soft, 1.5m/5ft tall, purple-flowering spires will hover serenely, complementing a haze of arching stems and flower spikes from the grasses. Has a refined profile in a herbaceous border, looks good next to the open, rose and rust-coloured flowers of *Echinacea purpurea*.

Buddleja davidii

A vigorous, moderately hardy, deciduous shrub that can be found growing out of guttering and from cracks in brickwork. Commonly known as the butterfly bush, owing to the strong attraction its summer-borne nectar has for a variety of butterflies. It is also popular with many other pollinating insects which makes it a candidate for a carefree wildlife garden. *B. davidii* 'Black Knight' has elegant, densely packed cone-shaped panicles of tiny, dark bluish purple flowers that give off a rich, sweet scent when they open in midsummer. Can be hard-pruned to maintain good flowers and foliage or allowed to grow into an open, natural shape up to 2.5m/8ft tall.

Campsis radicans

The common trumpet vine is a vigorous deciduous climber with large, 8cm/3in long, bright orange and scarlet funnel-shaped flowers that open in clusters of up to 12 blooms. The flowers, with their dense backdrop of coarsely toothed dark green compound leaves on woody twining stems, have a tropical, exotic look and bring colour into the garden when they appear in late summer and autumn. Once established, this is a very drought-tolerant climber that will reach up to 10m/30ft. Protect from severe frosts.

Glaucium flavum

A delicate coastal wildflower that grows conspicuously in barren stony ground. Yellow horned poppies look as if they haven't changed since they first evolved, the prehistoric simplicity of their pale bluish grey-green stems and crinkled fleshy foliage makes their delicate, open, papery yellow flowers –

borne in midsummer – appear all the more precious. The flowers don't last long in strong coastal gusts but, as the petals disappear, 30cm/12in long, thin, bean-like seedpods develop. You will often see immature flowers, open flowers and seedpods all on the one plant. A seaside beauty that likes its soil very poor and tolerates moderate winter frosts.

Gleditsia triacanthos 'Sunburst'

A golden form of the honey locust, this is a medium-sized, hardy, deciduous spreading tree with slightly contorted branches that create a delicate dappled shade of lacy shadows. It grows to a rounded, open shape when young before stretching to a more upright 12m/40ft profile with age. Slender snaking branches produce brilliant yellow-green, small-leaved foliage that can be regularly cut back to maintain bright, fresh leaves when the tree is young.

Lobelia tupa

A tough-looking coastal plant from the sandy slopes of South America that reaches up to 2.5m/8ft. Soft, furred, pale grey-green leaves crowd the lower parts of the many stems that push up and outwards from the base. These stems show a purple colouring as the leaves thin out towards the top where the fleshy, bright orange-red flowers – which are shaped like tiny flamingo beaks – open in panicles from midsummer to autumn. Works well in containers: try it next door to *Euphorbia mellifera* for an acid contrast. Thanks to its seaside origin, *L. tupa* is used to the comfort of winters without heavy frosts.

Perovskia 'Blue Spire'

This upright form of Russian sage is grown for its delicate, 1.2m/4ft tall stems of pale lavender-blue flowers. The lower parts of the stems are covered with regularly spaced, feathered grey-green leaves that have a sense of orderliness to contrast with the fine, open laciness of the flowering upper sections. Combines well with grasses and cottage garden perennials such as salvias, penstemons and campanulas. In winter its dried stems, if left out, make a beautiful framework for an icy coating of frost. Very hardy.

Phillyrea angustifolia
A densely foliated evergreen Mediterranean shrub with 8cm/3in long, narrow, pointed leaves of shiny dark green that can tolerate very cold winters. Grows to a slightly fluted shape but can appear quite natural and irregular, with the odd wayward stem pulling at its profile. Often used for clipping into topiary pieces such as balls, cubes and cylinders, it has green-ish white flowers that make up for their modest appearance with a rich fragrance in late spring. A hardy plant that grows to 3m/10ft, it is useful both as a windbreak and as a container-grown subject.

Ratibida columnifera
With flowers that resemble the small Mexican hats that give it its common name, this tough, hardy perennial adds colour to flowering grasses, cutting gardens and waning herbaceous bor-ders in late summer and early autumn. The flowers have a fat central column – at first green, then turning brown – that points skywards. From the bottom edge of this column a skirt or brim of yellow petals hangs down towards the greyish green basal leaves. The form *R. columnifera* f. *pulcherrima* has reddish brown hanging petals and grows slightly shorter than *R. columnifera*'s 80cm/2ft 8in.

Salvia sclarea
Clary sage has an aroma that some liken to cat urine – but this has never put me off. Firstly, because this description makes it sound far more unpleasant than the pungent lemony-pine aroma actually is and, secondly, because the rest of the plant is so bold and beautiful. Large, rough, mid-grey-green leaves expand and lean away from strong hairy stems as the plant

develops in late spring. From mid- to late summer, tall columns of flowering stems reach up to 1.2m/4ft and, in the variety *S. sclarea* var. *turkestanica*, open into pale blue flowers with lilac-white bracts that display a delicacy to counter the strong-looking foliage. Very hardy.

Santolina chamaecyparissus
Cotton lavender is a hardy shrub that forms mounds of rounded organic shapes and is often planted in a block as ground cover. There are those who snip off the bright yellow, rounded 1cm/½in summer-borne flowers so as not to detract from the undulating mass of silver-white, aromatic ever-green foliage that creates a seductive sculpted 50cm/20in thick carpet. This shrub can be clipped into low hedges to brighten a formal parterre, and is often planted in sunny cottage gardens where its flowers are a bright contrast to the blue of geraniums, lavender and perovskia.

Stipa gigantea
Dense, tufted evergreen clumps of slender grey-green leaves form the impenetrable base of this architectural perennial grass, protecting its roots in cold winters. The foliage keeps to a fairly uniform height of around 75cm/30in and acts as a launching pad for the towering 2.5m/6ft 6in stems that are sent up from midsummer, opening into metallic purplish green, oat-like flowers at their tips. The flower spikelets fade to a glowing golden yellow as they mature. This grass will appreciate a moderately fertile soil.

Tamarix ramosissima 'Rubra'
A large, deciduous shrub or small tree, whose slender reddish brown stems carry billowing plumes of needle-like grey-green foliage with racemes of rose-pink flowers that appear in late summer. Has a great tolerance of salt-laden, drying winds and makes a feathery hedge or windbreak, handy on exposed roof gardens. But its beauty

Salvia sclarea **var.** *turkestanica*

Glaucium flavum

Santolina chamaecyparissus

warrants more than a purely function-al role – try it as an individual feature plant to loosen the appearance of a sun-baked shrub border. For a structur-al profile, plant a row and allow it to grow unhindered into an informal hedge. For general good foliage, cut back hard in mid-spring.

Quick effects

Newly planted gardens can look bare and uninviting, but annuals, with their short, colourful lives, will plump up beds, soften hard edges and scamper up structures while the permanent planting develops.

Helianthus annuus

Brachyscome iberidifolia

The Swan River daisy is a drought-tolerant annual often grown in pots and window boxes where it forms a low, cushioned mass of feathery bright green foliage that fits itself around the stems of taller-growing plants such as osteospermums, French marigolds and gazanias. In summer, this foliage becomes star-spangled with a continuum of tiny daisy flowers that lean out towards the sunlight where they open purple before fading to a pale violet-tinged blue. Needs fertile, well-drained soil in a sunny spot.

Cosmos bipinnatus

Cosmos is a perfect solution for filling mid- and late-summer gaps in a herbaceous border as early-flowering perennials fade and go to seed. An upright-growing annual with branching feathery, fern-like foliage, *C. bipinnatus* throws a dash of colour wherever it is planted. Over a long period, a steady procession of 8cm/3in wide, flat-faced white, pink or crimson flowers with yellow centres are produced at heights of up to 1.5m/5ft. Deadhead regularly to maintain flowering and, in a random or carefree garden, leave a few flowers to self-seed at the end of the season. Plant in reasonably fertile soil in full sun.

Eschscholzia californica

Californian poppies are drought-tolerant, profuse-flowering annuals with white, yellow and pinkish red blooms that unfurl from pointed buds to single, open-faced flowers between spring and late summer. Once sown they are

hard to control, so best suit informal gardens where they can run around among grasses, pop up between slabs and along pathways and crop up in cracks along walls. Because they die at the end of every year, they shouldn't cause too much of an intrusion on your perennials, so cast some seeds along the edges of a mixed border or in containers where they will nestle and nudge their way between more solid plantings such as lavenders and salvias. They like a well-drained soil in full sun.

Helianthus annuus

Aside from their huge bright flowers, sunflowers are an extraordinary plant to include in your garden if only to witness how much one seed can grow in a matter of months. With a potential height of around 5m/15ft for the tallest varieties, these are a wonder to behold as their flowers open to a diameter of up to 30cm/12in. Loaded with seeds in the dark brown centre and surrounded with flaming, bright yellow petals, these are top of the list of favourite plants for children's gardens. Sunflowers are easily planted in containers as long as support is provided, with perhaps the shelter of a sunny wall. Provide a fertile, moist, well-drained soil – in full sun!

Ipomoea

A group of fast-growing climbers that will quickly latch hold of a fence, trellis or other structure with which their stems can entwine. *I. tricolor* (morning glory) scales objects up to 4m/13ft with dark green, heart-shaped leaves and produces a succession of intense,

azure-blue trumpet flowers 8cm/3in wide along its stems in mid- to late summer. *I. purpurea* 'Grandpa Otts' has sassy deep purple-blue trumpets with a star of pinkish lilac lines running into the centre. *I. lobata* (Spanish flag) is a more exotic alternative, with reddish stems and small fang-like flowers stacked up along an arching upright tip, at first opening red then fading through orange and yellow to white. Ipomoeas are grown as annuals as they need warm growing conditions and are cut back by frosts in winter. Start under glass and plant out once temperatures are warm in rich, well-drained soil in full sun.

Lathyrus odoratus

Sweet peas make a sprawling mass of twining flat-winged stems that, like their relatives in the vegetable garden, need support to get off the ground. A must for a romantic cottage-garden bower or arbour, where their scent will entrance, they also look good climbing up a hazel or metal obelisk – even a shrub such as buddleja, in a bed or border where their tremendous variety of colours can be better appreciated. They also grow well in pots where they can be enjoyed close up on a terrace or by a doorway. Reaching a height of 1.8m/6ft, they produce papery winged flowers in a colour range from magenta, scarlet, lilac and pink through blues to whites. Look in seed catalogues for the wide variety available. Plant in a rich, well-drained soil in full sun.

Eschscholzia 'Special Mixed'

Tropaeolum majus

Ricinus communis 'Impala'

Nicotiana

Grown as annuals, tobacco plants are popular for window boxes and pots as well as among perennials in borders. The greenish yellow or white star-shaped flowers of N. affinis are very fragrant, particularly at dusk, and open on 75cm/30in stems from midsummer to autumn. N. affinis 'Lime Green' has lime-green petals and N. x sanderae comes in red, pink, pale green and white. For a 1.5m/5ft tall, leafy tower, topped with long, scented white trumpets at the back of a shaded border, plant N. sylvestris where you have a spare 60cm/2ft of soil. Plant nicotianas as seedlings after the last frosts in fertile, well-drained soil in sun or shade.

Nigella damascena

Love-in-a-mist spreads a hazy mesh of feathery, bright green foliage that flows into the gaps between more rigid perennials and larger-leaved plants. This foliage collects in nest-like sprays around the base of its double star-shaped flowers with protruding stamens when they open in summer. N. damascena 'Miss Jekyll' has pale sky-blue flowers and grows to 45cm/18in; 'Oxford Blue' is a deeper, richer blue. Other varieties have pink, white and violet-blue flowers as well as mixtures of these colours in the 'Persian Jewel' series. All self-seed freely and will chart a random decorative course through your garden over the years if you allow them to. In spring, sow in situ in fertile, well-drained soil in full sun.

Oenothera biennis

A tall-growing biennial with reddish stems and red-veined green leaves that reaches up to 90cm/3ft. During the second half of summer at the top of these stems, 5cm/2in wide, cup-shaped, fragrant yellow flowers open at dusk – giving it its common name, evening primrose. Often found growing in the wild on waste ground or sandy soil along the coast, O. biennis seeds itself freely and looks good among ornamental grasses and other wild-flowers in a carefree design, or among the reclaimed objects and decorative dilapidation of a recycled garden. Can handle a poor, stony soil but needs sun.

Ricinus communis

The castor oil plant is an exotic, tropical-looking shrub, grown as an annual in cooler climates, with outlandish purple-brown, red-veined star-shaped leaves up to 45cm/18in across. Grown for its striking, glossy, tooth-edged foliage it combines stylishly with broad-leaved bananas and hedychiums to create a strong jungly feeling in an exotic planting. As it grows through summer, it becomes branched and spreading, reaching 1.8m/6ft tall with a spread of 1.2m/4ft. Plant in fertile, humus-rich soil in full sun. Note: all parts of this plant are toxic, so grow R. communis where it will not be a risk.

Rudbeckia hirta

Coneflowers make a bright, cheery splash of colour for containers and beds where their large daisy flowers – up to 13cm/5in wide – will crowd together in a busy cluster in the second half of summer. Annual, biennial or short-lived perennial, R. hirta reaches heights from 30–90cm/1–3ft, dependant on varieties, and comes in combinations of browns (R.h. 'Nutmeg'), orange (R.h. 'Marmalade'), even yellow and green (R.h. 'Green Eyes'). In most forms, the petals droop around the base of the central cone after a few days, so keep dead-heading for more blooms. Will grow in moist or dry soils in sun.

Tropaeolum majus

A rapid scrambling and climbing annual that can get up to 3m/10ft before the summer is out. Nasturtiums are a highly productive, self-reliant plant with rounded, wavy-edged bright green leaves up to 13cm/5in across that hover at different levels along the twining stems. During summer their tiered forms are ignited by many bright yellow and orange-red 5-petalled flowers that break out along their stems to glow within the foliage. Leaves and flowers have a hot, peppery taste when added to salads. The flowers draw predators and pollinators when planted in vegetable gardens. T.m. 'Empress of India' is an exotic bushy variety with dark purplish green leaves and deep scarlet flowers. Plant seeds in poorish soil and full sun.

Index

numbers in italic denote pictures

Acknowledgments

Author's Acknowledgments

Thank you Kirsten for looking after Rumi so lovingly over the past year, for tolerating my long hours lost in the attic at my keyboard and for insisting on dahlias – I agree, they really are the way forward. Thanks Mum for your weeding weekends and plant donations, and Dad for showing me New Zealand and for my row of radishes in the veg patch. Thanks also to Donald and Moss for patient company outdoors.

I have loved the adventure of putting these words to paper and greatly enjoyed working with so many people to bring this book to publication. I am especially grateful to the following for their invaluable support: my editor, Carole McGlynn, without whose wisdom, guidance and humour the process of writing my first book would have been twice as complicated and half as much fun. All involved at Frances Lincoln and in particular designer Jo Grey for so beautifully defining the style of the book, picture editor Anne Fraser for seeking out and marshalling so many photographs and my commissioning editor, Ginny Surtees, for inviting me to write.

I am grateful to Janice Pearce at Gardener's Palette and Tony Betteridge at Tendercare Nurseries for their generous advice and essential information at all hours, and to Sarah Morgan, Rafe Clutton, Virginia Nicholson, Olivier Bell and John Brown who allowed us to photograph in their gardens.

I am indebted to the many photographers whose beautiful images illustrate my text – especially Jerry Harpur, Steve Wooster, Andrea Jones, Michael Paul, Sunniva Harte and Clive Nichols who have all been more than generous.

I would also like to thank those with whom I have worked on gardens and enjoyed many laughs in recent years, especially Christopher Masson, Fergus Kinmonth, Chris Sykes, Jamie Owen, Simon Horton, Tessanna Hoare, Toby Hill, Anna Shepherd, Adrian Speed and Selina Fellows who got the whole thing started. I have always enjoyed my visits to Garden Books in London where Rob Cassy and Valerie Scriven have encouraged and fed my passion.

I am grateful to Heather de Haes, Mark Woloshyn, Pauline Griffiths, Christine Sullivan, Jill Sinclair, Richard Rudd, David Edgar at Flashback Television, Trevyn McDowell and the monks of Quarr Abbey for inviting me to realize my designs.

Thanks must go to the following suppliers who donated equipment for photography shoots: Haselden Enterprises (telephone: 01483 273 664) for hose reels and sprinklers; Spear and Jackson (www.spear-and-jackson.com) for hand tools; Felco (www.felco.ch) for secateurs and pruning equipment; Tina Knives for cuttings and grafting knives; The Recycle Works (www.recycleworks.co.uk) for Modular Compost Bins; and Haws Elliott (www.haws.co.uk) for metal watering cans.

And a final thank you to the *Guardian* for permitting us to reproduce certain passages.

Publishers' Acknowledgments

Commissioning editor   Ginny Surtees
Project editor   Carole McGlynn
Art editor   Jo Grey
Production   Kim Oliver
Picture editor   Anne Fraser

All artwork by Paul Thompson

Photographic Acknowledgments

a= above *b*=below *c*=centre *l*=left *r*=right *d*=designer

Nicola Browne: 4/5 and 13 (Peter Causer, East Sussex); 30/31 (d: Andrew Cao, Los Angeles); 40/41 (d: Naila Green); 76/77, 77*r* and 88*b* (Bertil Hanssen, Sweden); 108/109 (d: Avant Gardener, James Fraser, London). **Jonathan Buckley:** 63 (Gopsall Pottery, d: Michael Crosby-Jones); 82*b* and 104 ((Ketley's, East Sussex, d: Helen Yemm); 95*a* (d: Pedro da Costa Felgueiras, London). **Polly Farquharson**© FLL: 1. **Harpur Garden Library/Jerry Harpur:** 11, 87*ar*, 102*b* and 122/123 (Mr and Mrs Griffiths, d: Paul Thompson); 12, 25 and 112*a* (d: Luciano Giubbilei, London); 17, 89*ar* and 89*b* (d: John Douglas, Phoenix, Arizona); 20/21, 50 and 51 (Peter Causer, East Sussex); 28/29 and 29*r* (d: Martha Schwartz, Cambridge, Massachusetts); 34, 35 and 113*b* (San Diego Children's Hospital, d: Topher Delaney, San Francisco); 47*b* (d: Terry Welch, Seattle); 72, 73 and 93*al* (d: Steve Martino, Phoenix, Arizona); 74 and 75 (Villa La Casella, Alpes Maritimes); 78/79 (d: Richard Hartlage/Graeme Hardie); 83*b*, 89*ac* and 107*ar* (Jardin de Paradis, d: Eric Ossart & Arnaud Maurieres, France); 87*c* (d: Piet Oudolf, Hummelo, Holland); 113*a* (d: Christy Ten Eyck, Phoenix, Arizona); 166; 167*l* and *r*; 169*b*; 171*c*; 172*bl*; 175*c*; 179*a*; 181*br* and *bl*; 183*br*; 185*l* and *c*; 187*a*; 189*ar*; **/Marcus Harpur:** 106/107 (Garden in the Orchard, Norfolk); 165*ar*, *al*, and *br*; 167*c*; 175*r* and *l*; 177*a*; 179*c*; 183*a*; 185*r*; 187*c*; 188; 189*al* and *b*. **Sunniva Harte:** 6/7; 19 (d: Paul Thompson, East Sussex). **Andrea Jones:** 8, 14/15, 42/43 and 103*bl* (Trevyn McDowell, London, Channel 4 Garden Doctors, d: Paul Thompson); 15*a* (Jacob Marley, London, Channel 4 Garden Doctors, d: Paul Thompson); 60/61 (Gopsall Pottery, d: Michael Crosby-Jones); 82/83 (Neil Winder & Flo Maitland, Norfolk, Channel 4 Garden Doctors, d: Paul Thompson); 84*a* (d: Jim Buchanan); 162/163; Special Photography: 80/81, 86/87*b*, 114/5; 125*ar* and *b*; 127-137; 139*al*, *bl* and *r*; 140-153. **Ricardo Labougle:** 94/95. **Andrew Lawson:** 58 (d: James Fraser); 83*a* (d: June Summerhill); 110/111 (Hampton Court Flower Show 2000, d: Wynniatt-Husey Clarke); 165*bl*; 168; 169*a*; 171*a* and *b*; 172*a* and *br*; 177*b*; 179*b*; 181*a*; 183*bl*; 187*b*. **Marianne Majerus:** 18, 26/27*r* and *l* and 87*al* (d: Marc Schoellen); 52 to 55 d: Patrick Rampton); 56 and 57 (d: Susan Campbell);. **Clive Nichols:** 85*a* (d: Clare Matthews); 93*ar* (d: George Carter, Chelsea Flower Show 1999); 105*b* (Enköping, Sweden); 107*al* (d: Howitt/Bradstones/Chelsea Flower Show 2000); 109*a* and 139*ar* (d: Wynniatt-Husey Clarke, Regent's Park Flower Show 1999); 112/113*b* (Trevyn McDowell, London d: Paul Thompson). **Michael Paul:** 10; 16/*l* (d: Takao Habuka); 38 and 39 (d: Paul Thompson, East Sussex); 47*a*; 66/67 (Michael Pohl, d: Christopher Paul, NZ); 69 (Stable Courtyard Garden, Surrey, d: Anthony Paul); 95*br*; 111*ar* (d: Christopher Masson, Mauritian Garden Summer House). **Gary Rogers:** 44; 45 (d: Sandra Dana, Arizona); 86*a* (Athelhampton Gardens, Dorset); 88/89 (d: Henk Weijers, Holland); 90/91; 97*br* (d: Henk Weijers, Holland); 98/99*b*; 99*b* (d: Barbara Hammerstein); 100 (d: Elke & Siegfried Peters); 101*a* (Architect: Meyer-Jever); 101*br* (d: Ursula & Klaas Schnitzke-Spijker, Germany); 103*br* (d: Mary Keen); 105*a* (d: Ulrich & Hannalore Timm, Germany); 108*a* (d: Sandra Dana, Arizona). **Paul Thompson:** 116; 125*al*. **Juliette Wade:** 107*br* (Salvage Garden, Oxfordshire); 111*b* (Diana & Stephen Yakeley, London). **Steven Wooster:** 2/3 and 102/103 (Marge Perry, NZ); 32, 33, 84/85*b* and 101*bl* (d: Ivan Hicks, 'The Enchanted Forest', Groombridge Place, Kent); 36/37 (Tree Crop Farm, Akaroa, NZ); 48/49 (Titoki Point, NZ); 64/65 (Priona, Holland); 68 (d: Vivien Papich, Bellevue Gardens, NZ); 70/71 (d: Clive Higgie, NZ); 85*b* (Titoki Point, NZ); 91*br* (Di Firth, NZ) and *bl* (d: Michele Osbourne, London); 92/93*a* (Brinkhof Gardens, Holland); 92/93*b* (Barbara Lea Taylor, Akaroa, NZ); 96*a* (d: Anthony Paul) 96/97*b* (The Elliot's garden, Wainui Beach, NZ); 97*a* (Chaumont 9th International Garden Festival, d: Laurent Romanet, France); 98/99*a* (Priona Gardens, Holland); 103*a* (d: Vivien Papich, Bellevue Gardens, NZ); 109*b* (Meonstoke, NZ); 110*b* (Clive Higgie, NZ); 155-161; 176. **Elizabeth Whiting & Associates/Tim Street-Porter:** 16*r*.